Recovery of the
Protestant Adventure

RECOVERY of the PROTESTANT ADVENTURE

Neill Q. Hamilton

The Seabury Press / New York

The Seabury Press
815 Second Avenue
New York, N.Y. 10017

Library of Congress Cataloging in Publication Data

Hamilton, Neill Quinn.
    The recovery of the Protestant adventure.

    Includes bibliographical references.
    1. Bible. N.T. Mark—Criticism, interpretation, etc.
2. Protestant churches—United States. I. Title.
BS2585.2.H28   280′.4′0973   81-9121
ISBN 0-8164-2342-3 (pbk.)   AACR2

To the unknown disciples, clergy and lay, who steadfastly pursue the straight gate and narrow way of their discipleship within the institutional church—even when it feels more a burden than a help.

Contents

Acknowledgments

My gratitude extends to the many groups of theological students at Drew, and of laity and clergy in the churches, whose interest and criticism encouraged me to write down what began as conversations with them. At a crucial final stage, Mrs. Carolyn Fagan, theological student and administrative assistant to the director of the Multi-Ethnic Center, helped hugely with the final flurry of typing. My colleague, Professor S. Jan Forsythe Fishburn, generously read the whole and offered many valuable suggestions.

The one who actually produced the multiple drafts as well as providing unflagging support through the ups and downs of composition was Doris Kissling Hamilton. If her husband is ever known in the gates or sits among the elders of the land, it will be her doing as well as his. "Give her of the fruit of her hands and let her works praise her in the gates."

Introduction

This book aims at discovering what in the American world it means to be a Christian today, especially if you happen to be a Protestant. As I view the scene in the mainline Protestant denominations, there is no consensus about this. Instead, we are typically divided into two warring parties with very different ideas on the subject. These parties differ so strongly about the church's mission goals that they tend to immobilize the denominations they inhabit by the compromise they strike, because more often than not they agree to implement neither party's understanding of nurture or mission. We shall call these the private and the public parties in a conscious effort to avoid other labels.[1] The public party is convinced that the churches ought principally to aim at reforming the systems of society that tend to determine the spiritual life of individuals. If this is done, and maximum freedom is allowed the individual, salvation will somehow come to individuals, as well as to society.

On the other hand, the private party is convinced that if we concentrate on changing individual persons into Christians, and leave maximum liberty to social systems, the world will turn out to be the best possible under God. The public party advocates social action and prefers to leave individuals alone; the private party advocates evangelism and prefers to leave social systems alone. Each represents a kind of reverse image of the other, and church life tends to amount to a steady cold war between the two. Reports of church life in the daily paper keep us posted on how the war is going; the week in which I happen to be writing is typical. Sunday's *N.Y. Times* featured an article by the religious news editor entitled, "In Established Churches the Faithful are Restless."[2] Tuesday's edition reported that a bishop had been admitted to speak in a church of his diocese where he had been denied entrance a week before. This may be good copy, but it does not suggest an atmosphere attractive to people with serious religious interests.

Of course, Protestants do have some things in common, or we would not continue to gather so regularly. But some of what we share amounts to the saddest thing there is to know about us. Let recent research about Protestants speak for itself.

> We found from surveys of existing research, as well as from parts of our own studies, that commitments to religion and its expression as organized churches are important to many people, but generally are not ends in themselves. Instead, these commitments are often instrumental to attaining other goals to which people seem basically attached. These are: family, career, and standard of living, plus good health if that is at all a worry. If churches and church action are seen as supportive of good family life, an aid to the career, and no threat to the person's standard of living or health, then commitment to the church can be high. There is also an intrinsic "religious need" motivation for church commitment for many people. But if church beliefs or actions are seen as undermining any of the Big Three basic American values, commitment to the church is weakened drastically for most people. Even intrinsic motivation will not persist.[3]

This suggests that whatever Protestants profess to be about, we are mainly engaged in some kind of folk religion—something that would perhaps suffice for those who need minor assurance in the face of the trivial uncertainties in daily living. But for those who feel their lives at stake in the search for the straight gate and narrow way, it is not an encouraging atmosphere. Indeed, declining church membership suggests that we do not appear to be even *interesting* to a majority of Americans, who must perceive us to be too little different from everyone else for the commitment of church membership to be worth their trouble. We Protestants have lost the sense of who we are and what we ought to be up to. Until we recover that sense, we will neither attract others to join with us nor convene caring, adventurous communities that might point the way to a more hopeful future for all.

Our Protestant ancestors received their identity by experiencing a divine call. We, their descendants, need that same identity-granting experience. To have it, we must put ourselves within hearing range of God's voice. We begin to come into range as we recall and act on the conviction of all Christians in the Great Tradition that at one time, in one particular set of circumstances, God spoke in a way that revealed and defined who we are intended to be. That time was the period of the writing of the New Testament; the circumstances were those represented in the New Testament writings.

The New Testament is the definitve witness to the divine self-disclosure in the person of Jesus Christ. Divine self-disclosure is also the disclosure of what it is to be truly human. Therein lies the authority of the New Testament writings as the source for the recovery of Christian identity. God, who is the Father of our Lord and Savior, Jesus Christ, for a certainty spoke in these writings, and this same God continues to speak through their witness. The New Testament is where to go to listen for the "call."

But God spoke then in timely accord with the circumstances and settings peculiar to the various New Testament writings, and this produced a variety of forms of God's call. Recognition of that variety is important, because it points to the gracious character of the One who speaks; for in speaking, God accommodates to hearers in their particular situations. We are thus encouraged to expect that God has something special to say to us, in our particular plight.

This variety in forms of "call" has caused anxiety among some Christians, who seem to wish that God had spoken more monotonously. To remedy the presumed defect, they attempt to reduce the New Testament witness to the single form of a particular confessional or theological system. A casual, unprejudiced reading of the New Testament and a modest knowledge of the history of its compilation should make it obvious that the New Testament will not tolerate such reduction.[4] If variety of forms of witness makes us anxious, we may find reassurance in the steady character of the God who speaks in the midst of all the variety. God remains true to God while speaking to the situation of each hearer. This way that God has of speaking in accord with the situation of the hearer suggests the next step toward drawing within hearing range of God's call.

We need to choose one New Testament book and begin to listen to the call there. Since God speaks to situations, we are most likely to hear a word for our own time when we choose a book with a situation similar to our own. By noting the way in which our situation matches that of the community of the New Testament book, what was said to them comes to bear on us. For us, this shall be the Gospel of Mark.

There is a time-tested way to grasp both the New Testament book's situation and our own; it is called the historical-critical method. Any human situation is a momentary point in the ongoing sweep of events we call history. Our situations are always a composite of the previous flow of formative events and our past—and continuing—response to them. Ordinarily we are not aware of this flow and response: we are too occupied with the everyday tasks of coping. When, however, we step aside from these to observe the flow over a given period, we become aware of our history. That is the historical side of the method. The "critical" side has to do with deciding which events in the flow have been most formative and what the pattern of crucial responses has been. This discriminating awareness of flow and response is the key to discovering situations both in the New Testament book and in our own lives.

Applied to ourselves, this careful, discriminating review of how we got to where we are implies some evaluation of what we have been doing. That may seem to add still another task to the burden of daily life and make us reluctant to begin the review at all. But there are times in our lives when it does not seem worthwhile to continue without a critical review. That is the point, it seems to me, American Protestantism has reached.

In the measure that other American religious communities feel the need to renew their sense of identity and mission, some appreciation of the Protestant experience is probably indispensable. One reason is because the melting pot of American culture tends to melt down all distinctive religious identities to the point that being "American" overwhelms everything else. The fate of Protestants ought to illumine this assimilation for all, and the process for recovering should be helpful as well. Another reason is that since Protestantism has been the dominant religious influence within American culture until well past the turn of the century, to some degree all other Americans have had to forge their identities in a context fundamentally shaped by Protestantism. Americans of whatever stripe understand themselves better when they gain clarity about the developments in American Protestantism.

As I read the Protestant story in America, I find that at its core it has always sought to be a faithful biblical people. If we undertake the pilgrimage back to our canonical roots in the way I shall try to suggest, we will fall in with our sisters and brothers in all the family branches of Christianity as pilgrims on the same journey. I devoutly expect that when we all return, we shall not be merely more Protestant or more Catholic, but more Christian. Herein lies the hope of healing the great wound in the body of Christ, that well-traveled Christians discover their spiritual homes in Jerusalem, though their local addresses remain Rome, Geneva, or Constantinople.

Part I

The Collapse of the Protestant Adventure

...rather I wrote to you not to associate with any one who bears the name of brother if he is guilty of immorality or greed...not even to eat with such a one.

The Apostle Paul 1 Corinthians 5:11

Neither the Church of Christ, nor a Christian Commonwealth ought to tolerate such as prefer private gain to the public weal, or seek it to the hurt of their neighbors.

Bucer, De Regno Christi

Capitalism is the extraordinary belief that the nastiest of men for the nastiest of motives will somehow work for the benefit of us all.

John Maynard Keynes

·1·

The European Prelude

It is relatively more difficult to disclose our own situation as American Protestants than to put a New Testament book into its historical setting. Unfortunately, a discriminating awareness of the American Protestant experience is too little emphasized in the nurture of the churches and in the pecking order of theological education. Sidney Mead, an authority in American Church History, shared his experience of how little church history theological students actually learn.

> European Biblical and Theological scholarship, . . . has largely dominated our theological education for a hundred years. At least in my experience most of the seminary graduates who have come to me for graduate work in American Church History confess that they know practically nothing about the American experience of Christianity and its consequent modes of thinking and acting.[1]

The fact that clergy have not learned to think critically and historically about modes of thinking and acting present in American churches helps explain why so many laity read their own prejudices into the Bible. Long experience as a teacher of Bible leads me to begin this book with our situation. Protestants always emphasize the primacy of the Bible in their nurture—Protestants, after all, are biblical people. Accordingly, Protestants, of whatever persuasion, are taught that their favorite convictions are biblical, although they may have little first-hand knowledge of the Bible. So when Protestants do open the Bible they are condemned by their nurture to confirm their prejudices. When I teach the New Testament, in seminary or out, that is what I see happen constantly. Only an informed awareness of how our prejudices arose, can free the Bible to correct them.

Professor Mead serves notice that the path to the awareness we seek winds through a great deal of new information. That could mislead us into supposing that the path to awareness is primarily a head trip. Nothing could be further from the truth. It is primarily a consciousness-raising trip in which the information provides a springboard to new perspectives, new realizations, and new feelings about who we really are in contrast to the way we are accustomed to seeing and feeling our identity as American Protestants.

Reformation and the Ascetic Ideal

The American Protestant experience began, like all Protestantism, with the Reformation. It is useful to follow the suggestion that, at heart, the Protestant adventure was a kind of inner-worldly asceticism.[2] Christian asceticism had been brought to a fine art by the monastic orders of the medieval church. Their aim was to live out the gospel way of life completely—to follow the counsels of perfection suggested by verses like Matthew 19:21, "...If you would be perfect, go, sell what you possess and give to the poor..." and Matthew 5:48, "You, therefore, must be perfect as your heavenly Father is perfect." This perfection could only be found, according to monastic theory, by withdrawal from worldly activities such as earning a living in the marketplace, marrying, and raising a family. The monastic way of life was eventually distilled into the triple vows of poverty, chastity, and obedience. The way of perfection was not for everyone, but only for those specially called.

But only those were truly religious who did follow the

counsels of perfection. Consequently "the religious" became the title for those who entered the orders. All other Christians were second-class citizens of the kingdom and depended for their salvation on the sacramental system and the treasury of merit accumulated by the truly "religious."[3]

Worldly Asceticism

By protesting the nonbiblical character of the monastic vows, the idea of merit associated with them, and the sacramental system that provided the context for both monastics and lay Christians, the Reformation closed the door on monasticism and opened a door to the world. It intended, however, to continue the ascetic spirit of the orders by carrying the same degree of devotion and commitment practiced in the seclusion of monasteries out into the everyday round of work and family life. In sympathy with this way of looking at the Protestant adventure, H. Richard Niebuhr once compared the American denominations to the old monastic orders. "These Pilgrims, Congregationalists, Quakers, Baptists, these Mennonites, these Disciples and Christians— what are they but Protestant orders.... and Methodist preachers, with their saddle bags and books of discipline, are Franciscans and Dominicans in a new incarnation."[4]

Although the medieval church judged the world an unfit place for perfect discipleship, it did not consider it beyond the bounds of divine regulation. God ruled the world through natural law. By coupling God's law revealed in Scripture with God's law revealed in nature, the church gave minute direction to every activity in society. The Calvinist wing of the Reformation continued this view of the world as a place amenable to godly regulation. It emphasized the idea of the overarching, all-encompassing sovereignty of God from which even a fallen and corrupted world could not escape. Calvinism was the most important religious influence for the American experience, since by way of Puritans as well as non-English heirs of Calvin, an estimated eighty to ninety percent of revolutionary America bore the "stamp of Geneva" in its moral and religious heritage.[5]

This special understanding of the relation of God to the world led to features of Calvinistic piety that became formative for the American experience. One such feature was the heavily calculating character of worldly asceticism as distinguished from the contemplative bent of other-worldly asceticism. According to Calvinism, the peak experience of life is not to see God in an ineffable vision, but to bring glory to God by making the human will an instrument of the divine purpose in every detail of common life. To the Calvinist, piety was essentially obedience. Concentration on organizing the will meant a corresponding turning away from intuition, feeling, and spontaneity.

As the Calvinist saint addressed the world, he was presented with a variety of possible points of entry. He needed a sense of direction from God comparable to the special guidance which the monk or nun had received. This led to the doctrine of the calling.[6] According to this idea, God has a slot in the work-a-day world which it is each person's calling to fulfill by divine appointment. It is second in importance only to the call to become a Christian. And except for the special activities related to the worship of God, Christians fulfill their destiny by scrupulous devotion to that calling. In 1678 Richard Baxter put it this way,

> Be wholly taken up in diligent business of your lawful callings, when you are not exercised in the more immediate service of God.[7]

Thus work became a divine duty. Of course, it had a utilitarian function as part of the divine plan to provide for the needs of society. But the main importance of work stemmed not from its products, but from its appointment by God as the main vehicle of working out one's salvation in the world. One could say for Calvinist Protestants that work became their third sacrament.

A Careful Compromise with Capitalism

In Calvin's concept of a worldly calling as the arena in which the believer lived out obedience to God, a crucial compromise with reference to the use of capital was made. In medieval social ethics, lending money at interest was usury, and was forbidden by divine law. Because of an economic revolution that led to the formation of a rising middle class in the early sixteenth century, Calvin accepted capitalism as an arrangement congenial to a calling under certain circumstances. While breaking with medieval social ethics, Calvin carefully circumscribed the new freedom concerning the use of money.

> That interest is lawful, provided that it does not exceed an official maximum, that, even when a maximum is fixed, loans must be made *gratis* to the poor, that the borrower must reap as much advantage as the lender, that excessive security must not be exacted, that what is venial as an occasional expedient is reprehensible when carried on as a regular occupation, that no man may snatch economic gain for himself to the injury of his neighbor—a condonation of usury protected by such embarrassing entanglements can have offered but tepid consolation to the devout money-lender.[8]

The point is not so much the new freedom, for it was narrow enough, but the break with medieval social policy which it represented. Capital, credit, and banking now became acceptable. The standard for income was no longer merely whatever subsistence called for. Middlemen ceased being parasites, and loans at interest, thievery. Profits from trade and finance became as respectable as the wages of a laborer. This new status accorded to conventional business activity made it possible for members of the rising middle class to strive for sainthood, while remaining middle class.

It is difficult for the modern Protestant to see this critical step made by Calvin in its proper perspective. There was no license to conduct business as one pleased, such as we contemporary Protestants consider our due. Autonomy in business was for Calvinistic devotees of the sovereignty of God as unthinkable as autonomy in any other area of personal or social life. The premise of medieval social policy had been that society was an integrated organism. In it, economic interests were subordinate to the real end of life—salvation. Economic conduct was simply one aspect of personal conduct upon which, of course, the rules of conduct were binding. Unrestrained economic appetite was just as unthinkable as unrestrained aggression or unrestrained sexuality. Calvin fully endorsed this point of view. Still, since the Calvinist economic ethic was first worked out in a middle-class situation, there was a special affinity between Calvinism and the middle class which has continued into the American Protestant experience.[9]

Puritan Variations on Calvin

During the century between the early Calvinism of Calvin's Geneva and the Calvinism brought to America by English Puritans in the 1630s, English Puritanism added elements to Calvin's social ethic. The English version of Calvinism provided a preview of what happens when the spirit of the middle class overwhelms the Protestant spirit.

The Calvinist heritage of Geneva was a two-pronged enterprise: to have a personal experience of God's saving grace and to live it out in the world through the calling via worldly asceticism. Although Calvin paid scant attention to spiritual experience, the Puritan movement filled this gap by recovering the mystical, contemplative element of monastic piety that gave Puritanism an introspective cast. "Puritans . . . came increasingly to regard a specific experience of regeneration as an essential sign of election."[10]

A century of refining the Calvinistic tradition in Puritan England not only clarified the inner dimension of worldly asceticism, it also molded the external shape of life in the worldly calling. English Puritanism culminated in "the triumph of the economic virtues."[11] In Calvin's time, at the launching of worldly asceticism, Protestants committed themselves to an exploration of the notion that the qualities that led to success in business might turn out to be comfortable companions to more distinctly Christian virtues. Those qualities were: thrift, diligence, sobriety, and frugality. They were the qualities of the middle class at its best. Compared to the "quarrelsome, self-indulgent nobility" and to "the extravagant and half-bankrupt monarchies" of the time, these were virtues indeed.

As everyone knew from the beginning, worldly asceticism involved risk. Daniel had been compelled to enter the lion's den; Calvinists and Puritans took up lion taming as a profession. With such a vocation, one hopes not to be mauled, let alone devoured. The story of English Puritanism, alas, ended with this latter indignity.

The Collapse of the Reformation Ideal

Not long after the Puritan exodus to America, English Puritan resistance to avarice and private economic ambition collapsed, and economic virtues triumphed over Christian ones. The Genevan program had projected a personal reformation of character carried out in a reformed social order designed to embody the same values in both spheres. With the 1660 Restoration in England, a reaction to the social side of Puritan virtue set in. The typical Puritan capitulated to this reaction by divorcing private life, which continued to be pious, from public life. This epidemic of indifference to the common good spawned the callousness toward the inhumanities of the early Industrial Revolution described by Dickens. Intense preoccupation with individual religious experience and individual salvation, plus everyday familiarity with the single-minded acquisitive spirit of financial capitalism, made the collapse of the original piety understandable, even predictable.

It will be important to remember that this possibility was also part of the heritage of the American Protestant. The double emphasis in early Calvinism on individual piety and social responsibility is the distinctive feature of the Protestant adventure. The collapse of the social ethic in English Puritanism can be traced to the fact that the distinctive note in English Puritanism was individual responsibility without the companion emphasis on social responsibility characteristic of the Calvinist form of the Protestant adventure.

·2·

American Puritans and the Great Awakening (1725–1750)

Jonathan Edwards, the Archetype

When English Puritans arrived in America, they were still as dedicated to building a Christian world as they were to forming individual Christians. It seemed that Providence had given them a free hand to do just that in fresh, unorganized territory. If Europe had successfully resisted Protestant asceticism in its attempt to turn the old world into a kind of Puritan monastery, perhaps the new world would be more amenable. Consequently, Puritans set out to establish a "Bible commonwealth" in New England. This attempt to found a Christian society in New England was an extension of the Puritan project to make England Christian.

A minister in the Bay Colony summarized the project: "Christ reigns among us in the commonwealth as well as in the Church and hath his glorious interest involved and wrapped up in the good of both societies respectively."[1] The church in that colony pioneered a new shape of the divine community by being the first state church to require an experience of grace for membership. The classic double-pronged Calvinist enterprise was faithfully launched—converted, visible saints in a society ruled by the law of God.

If Puritans from England continued the same project in the

new world, they could expect the same opposition that had scuttled the project at home. The new settlers had come, after all, under the auspices of companies which hoped for commercial gain. As time went by, it became obvious that the colonists were a cross section of the English among whom Puritans were a minority. Their clergy often observed that the majority seemed chiefly interested in making money. There were plenty of professing Christians but they were failing to qualify for church membership because of the requirement to give a creditable account of their conversion.

The worldly asceticism preached by Puritan clergy met especially successful resistance in the Boston area. As early as 1630, a self-conscious merchant class had opposed the interpretation of the Bible by the clergy as too restrictive of healthy commerce. In the rechartering of the Bay Colony in 1691, the right to vote came to be based on property rather than upon church membership. They welcomed the new charter which improved the commercial situation.

In 1699, the merchants took a further step toward dilution of the Puritan ethos. Under the leadership of John Leverett, and William and Thomas Brattle, the church issued a "manifesto" with startlingly lax membership arrangements. A perfunctory profession of faith replaced earlier requirements that the potential communicant give a satisfactory account of conversion. All who contributed to the support of the minister had a voice in his hiring and firing. To further consolidate their ascendancy over clerical influence, they deposed Increase Mather in 1701, and in 1707 installed their own leader, John Leverett, a layman, as president of Harvard. Thus ended the reign of Harvard as a fountainhead of inconvenient piety. From that time onward, Massachusetts fostered a more worldly than ascetic version of Protestantism as distinct from the classic heritage.

Did the resistance to worldly asceticism in Massachusetts represent a general slide backward toward the worldliness of Restoration England, which in 1660 had seen a general repudiation of Puritan piety? Had the reaction only been delayed by the novelty of the colonial situation? Was it humanly impossible to keep the original fervor of the Protestant adventure, or had the medieval church been more realistic? By way of reply Protestantism in America invented a device to keep its history holy. It was the "awakening." It first appeared in America in the form of the Great Awakening, 1725–1750.[2]

The First Awakening

The Great Awakening represented the first major adjustment of the European Protestant experience to the new American circumstances. The move on the part of the Boston merchants, though doubtless frustrating to their clerical contemporaries, heralded the arrangement to come. It announced that the church establishment and clerical domination of the church would not work in America. The democratic thrust of Protestant theology, the leveling effect on class of a pioneering situation, and the weakening of tradition, did not accord well with the imposed, authoritarian style of European church management.

At the time, the Great Awakening appeared to be a miraculous intervention of God working through the preaching of Solomon Stoddard in Connecticut, his grandson Jonathan Edwards in Massachusetts, the Tenant brothers in New Jersey, and the English evangelist George Whitfield, to revitalize a declining Puritan piety. Viewed in historical perspective, the Awakening marks the beginning of an enduring cleavage in the American Protestant experience between faith and reason, head and heart, expressed as opposing rather than complementary emphasis in subsequent theological parties.

The Awakening marks a turning point as Puritan piety was adapted to the American experience through the use of Enlightenment thought forms that displaced the biblical and theological thought forms of the Puritan world view. The life and thought of Jonathan Edwards (1703–1758) is typical of changes occurring in church life and in theology as the Puritan adventure was domesticated by the American experience.

By the 1730s the Puritan standard for church membership was impossible to maintain in a land where dissenters, like the merchants, were free to found a church to their own liking. Consequently, when Edwards, inspired by the spiritual powers evident in conversions of the Awakening, attempted to reinstitute the practice of confessing conversion as the standard for church membership, he was asked to resign from his Northampton pulpit. Edwards' misfortune marks the decline of clergy authority in matters theological and ecclesiastical, and the beginning of a style of evangelical consensus still normative in Protestant denominations.

The denomination was itself a product of the Awakening. Its genius was that it provided a variety of ways of being Protestant without one way having to declare that the other ways were not the true church. This arrangement was made possible because the common Awakening experience cut across religious, class, and geographical differences. In the process it confirmed the cultural establishment of Calvinistic Protestantism as the dominant religious influence in the American experience. As the first pan-colonial experience in America, it staked a Protestant claim that would become influential during the Revolution.

Jonathan Edwards emerged as the great theologian of the Awakening as he adapted his Puritan heritage to the issues posed by the "mighty acts of God." Like many of his peers, he saw the Awakening as a sign of the nearness of the millennium in America, a sign that this was an elect people, and America, the promised land.

> America has received the true religion of the old continent,...and inasmuch as that continent crucified Christ, they shall not have the honor of communicating religion in its most glorious state to us but we to them...When God is about to turn the earth into a Paradise, he does not begin his work where there is some good growth already, but in a wilderness...that the light may shine out of darkness, and the world be replenished from emptiness.[3]

In asserting that the new promised land had received the

true religion, Edwards followed his Puritan predecessors in assuming that only English civilization was an adequate vehicle for the purpose of God. Although Edwards spent his next years as a missionary to native Americans, his theology presupposes that since native Americans and blacks were not English by heritage they could not belong to the elect through whom God was to fulfill the plan of salvation in history. Even conversion did not change the status of such people. This unstated dogma that the English form of civilization had an exclusive place in redemptive history would continually haunt and distort the American Protestant experience.

Capitulation to the Enlightenment

When Edwards wrote his major theological treatise, *The Religious Affections*, he was influenced by the psychology and social philosophy of John Locke. Although Edwards remained true to Puritan distinctions between the elect and nonelect as he provided guidelines to discern whether an "awakening" experience was a genuine conversion or not, he was subtly shaped by the more scientific mode of thought found in Locke and Enlightenment philosophy. Edwards reveled in the scientific experiment as an expression of the wonders made evident in God's world.

Clergy of Edwards' generation generally took little account of the challenge of the Enlightenment to theology and the redefinition of society and of social responsibility implied in it. They recognized the challenge quickly enough when it took the form of Deism. What they and too few others recognized was that the Enlightenment offered to exchange the medieval-Reformation view of an organic, personally and morally interdependent society for a mechanistic, mathematically interrelated one which worked out its own salvation automatically and inevitably without the ancient inconveniences of neighborly concern and divine solicitude. One of the first places this new view found expression was in the realm of economics.

After the English Restoration in 1660, the Protestant

adventure had collapsed in capitulation to economic individualism so that, according to Tawney, "...the attempt to maintain the theory that there was a Christian standard of economic conduct was impossible..."[4] The Enlightenment filled the void left by the obsolescence of the medieval-Reformation view of economic relations and responsibilities. One suspects that for many it was a planned obsolescence. As Tawney puts it,

> The future for the next two hundred years is not the attempt to reaffirm, with due allowance for altered circumstances, the conception that a rule is binding on Christians in their economic transactions, but with the new science of Political Arithmetic, which asserts, at first with hesitation and then with confidence, that no moral rule beyond the letter of the law exists. Influenced in its method by the contemporary progress of mathematics and physics, it handles economic phenomena, not as a casuist, concerned to distinguish right from wrong, but as a scientist, applying a new calculus to impersonal economic forces. Its method, temper, and assumptions are accepted by all educated men, including the clergy, even though its particular conclusions continue for long to be disputed.[5]

In the place of the early Puritan dedication to building a Christian world as they were forming individual Christians, the chief end of government in Lockean social philosophy was the preservation of property. No longer was the government of the commonwealth the servant of a social order meant to serve "the glorious interest...of Christ." As John Locke put it, "The great and chief end, therefore, of men uniting into Commonwealths and putting themselves under government is the preservation of their property..."[6]

The principle is softened by the context in that "property" is defined to include preservation of life, liberty, and estates. Still, the summary term Locke chose is symptomatic. At the time of the Great Awakening, the culture to which America was granting divine rights was well on its way to the construction of a Western counterpart to the Eastern cyclical universe. In the Eastern version, a series of reincarnations handles the problem of social justice automatically. In repeated returns to earth in varying forms, fate grants each individual the precise level of well-being deserved regardless of social systems. Thus, a deeply religious and compassionate devotee of reincarnation can meditate in complete composure while within the sound of his chant, neighbors die in the street outside, smoke from his incense mingling with their dying breath. The Western version, while following a linear, this-worldly model, can provide the Western saint with equivalent insulation. A mathematically reliable economic system that distributes well-being with automatic justice offered to deliver the Enlightenment saint from the nagging concern for the less fortunate neighbor that so preoccupied all of his Christian forebears.

Just as the convergence of the events of the Awakening with Enlightenment thought altered the early Puritan social ethic, the same convergence gradually altered the understanding of human agency in the conversion process. Solomon Stoddard, the precursor and catalyst in New England of the Great Awakening, accentuated human agency as part of his attempt to arrest the decline of the church. He advocated abandonment of church covenants, more effective preaching, and use of the Lord's Supper as an aid to conversion. In his preaching, he held up the threat of final judgment upon each individual, rather than upon the community. Stimulated by the prospect of judgment, the candidate for salvation was moved to act. Before his death in 1729, Stoddard's policies had led to five revivals in western Massachusetts and Connecticut.[7]

The Awakening made revivalism an especially American institution. It had showed that Christianity would advance in America, not through old-world style religious establishments, but through voluntary associations of individuals who had experienced the converting work of the Spirit.

Great Awakening churches were content for their membership to be a minority of the population, although an estimated twenty to fifty thousand were added to the churches. With so many having actually experienced regeneration, the idea of a converted membership was renewed. Though converted church members were relatively few in the population as a whole, the Calvinist-Puritan heritage of the "calling" coupled piety with common life so effectively that the Awakening translated immediately into civic institutions with an impact out of all proportion to the number actually converted. This disproportionate impact was aided by the fact that the Awakening· refused to conform to the class-bound character of European Puritanism. "Though young people may have been especially numerous among new converts, it [the Awakening] attracted or repelled people of every class and station, rural and urban, young and old, and in every region."[8]

The Great Awakening was a remarkably effective response of American Protestantism to the challenge to adapt its Calvinist spirit to the American situation. In the process, the English Puritan emphasis on spiritual experience and piety was transformed into a conversion experience related more to revival preaching than to the life of the congregation. The Calvinist concern with social justice in the interest of "the common good" was replaced by an ethic related to the acts of the converted which served as evidence that the experience had been genuine. The understanding of the "calling" and the use of money as related to "the common good" gradually became individual rather than communal concerns. Early Puritan communalism was giving way to religious individualism and social indifference.

·3·

The Second Great Awakening (1795–1835)

Finney, the Archetype

"Great" means broad in scope, that is, nationwide. "Awakening" means "a theological reorientation that coincided with an intellectual and social reorientation in such a way as to awaken a new interest in the Christian ethos which underlies American civilization."[1] The post-Revolutionary decades were a crisis period for the churches. Distraction from churchly business that naturally accompanies war was aggravated by the fact that the founding of the new nation was as much a triumph for the Enlightenment as it was for Protestantism. If the first national heroes were leaders of the Great Awakening, the next national heroes, Washington, Jefferson, Franklin, and Paine, were leaders of an Enlightenment awakening. The disestablishment of the churches by the First Amendment left Protestants with a strong impression of their minority status. They met the challenge with the Second nationwide Awakening.

As the nineteenth century opened, Protestant church membership was somewhere between four and seven percent of the population.[2] The end of the Second Awakening saw a doubling of that proportion. If one counts the active constituency as well as formal members, the adjusted proportions in terms of the church membership requirements of today would turn out to be something like an increase from forty percent of the population to seventy-five percent. It was enough of a change to lead into "the most Protestant period in America."

Revivalism

The change was wrought through revivals that began in the camp meetings of Tennessee and Kentucky. The symbol of that phase was the camp meeting at Cane Ridge, Kentucky, where an estimated ten to twenty thousand camped out for six or seven days of dawn-to-campfire evangelism beginning on August 6, 1801. That revived revivalism and defined the technique for evangelizing the western fringes of the new nation. Baptists and Methodists were especially skilled at creating revivals on the frontier. That skill so launched Methodist growth, that by 1844 it had become the largest denomination in America. From 1800 to 1830, it grew from 30,000 to more than 175,000. The place of revivalism in the American Protestant experience was established. Those who, like Methodists, went with it, multiplied. Those who, like Presbyterians, hesitated, slumped. But the method of revivalism was not the only factor in the special appeal of Methodism. Its message further adjusted the Puritan-Calvinist theology to the American experience. That shift was characteristic of Second Awakening theology. The shift was especially clear in the emergence of "the New Divinity" in the New England phase of the Awakening.

The "New Divinity" was also called the New Haven theology. Revivals swept central and western New York in 1800. In 1802, a revival at Yale led to professions of conversion by one third of the student body. Two Yale graduates, Lyman Beecher and Nathaniel W. Taylor, led the New England Awakening; more particularly, their theology did. Taylor remained in the Calvinistic tradition but made sin voluntary. The contention was that sinners had "power to the contrary," that is, the ability to resist saving grace. By granting a larger role to human ability, Taylor not only put into sinners' hands new ability to respond to the gospel, he also put into evangelists' hands the power to arrange revivals. The day of waiting helplessly for a regenerating experience, or for a revival, was over. Both came to depend on human agency, assuming God's cooperation. The Westminster Confession had been Americanized. Beecher, the great practitioner of Taylor's theology, achieved outstanding success as a revival preacher-pastor. He led the evangelicals to greater influence in Boston than the Unitarians.[3]

Finney's Indigenous Theology

But the theological line opened up by Taylor, and implemented in ministry by Beecher, was to be carried forward with a logical consistency that shocked them both. The ultimate American revivalist, who adjusted the evangelical heritage to the American experience with rigorous consistency, was Charles Finney. A practicing lawyer with a profound conversion experience, Finney began his evangelistic ministry without the restraining grace of a formal theological education. That left him free to filter the Bible and current theology through a brilliant mind, completely molded by optimistic, rationalistic, commonsense, Enlightenment logic. That mindset, coupled with an intense religious experience, matched perfectly the dominant mood of American culture. No wonder his message and methods moved his hearers so dramatically. Finney was the archetype of the indigenous American evangelical. He taught the New Haven theology with a consistency that startled its founders. Beecher had been shifting the heritage of Jonathan Edwards in New England toward the commonsense logic of the times with caution and subtlety, in hopes that fellow clergy would hardly notice and that the Congregational-Presbyterian alliance would remain undisturbed. Finney threw caution to the winds, alarming the Princetonian Presbyterians. Presbyterian tradition made it shy both of Finney's means and message. But the times were with Finney.

Two major adjustments to traditional Calvinism grounded Finney's theological position.[4] The first was a displacing of emphasis on the glory of God with "disinterested benevolence." The term was adapted from Edward's theology by his student Samuel Hopkins, who stressed the love of neighbor as the equivalent of love of "Being in general", that is, God. "Disinterested benevolence" was further refined to the "greatest good of mankind" and finally allied with "the pursuit of happiness." Accordingly, Finney could say, "Look at the utility of benevolence." "If we desire the happiness of others, their happiness will increase our own, according to the strength of our desire." Whoever dedicated his or her self to disinterested benevolence, served at once the good of neighbor, one's own happiness, and the glory of God. Indeed, the reign of God equalled the reign of disinterested benevolence.

Along with this adjustment of the glory of God came an adjustment of the role granted to human ability. Knowing that disinterested benevolence summarized the whole of true religion, could human beings act on that knowledge? In his programmatic sermon, "Sinners Bound to Change Their Own Hearts," Finney answered, "Yes." There was nothing *constitutionally* wrong with human beings as a result of Adam's sin. They were prejudiced by self-interest and ignorance. Once ignorance had been removed by preaching and the clear alternative of disinterested benevolence explained, all people had the inherent ability to decide for benevolence and thus "to change their own hearts." It irritated Finney to preach to captives of Calvinism who met his command to decide with the plea that they could not. According to Finney, they could, and they must. Finney put people through a two-stage experience. He first threatened them with the wrath of God for their prejudice and ignorance. When thoroughly aroused by the "animal feelings," he shifted to a wooing encouragement, an appeal to what he called "religious affections." This was a plea to act on the ability all possessed to choose benevolence. Yielding to the plea of "religious affections" produced an overwhelming sense of relief in direct proportion to the terror of "animal feelings." The shift from one to the other became the evangelical experience. Finney's fantastic success in mediating this experience was offered as proof of the truth of this theology, a claim that seemed to satisfy the intuitional, experiential side of the American character.

In addition, Finney complemented the appeal from experience with the appeal to the "laws of the mind," thus reconciling religion with the growing American faith in science. Just as the new science was producing a new philosophy of a mechanized universe, Finney appealed to a similar model to explain and engineer religious response. We have noted how this world view produced an arithmetic of economics; Finney's theology verged on being an arithmetic of religion. "When the blessing evidently follows the introduction of the measure itself, the proof is unanswerable that the measure is wise." Thus, success measured by the number of converts is a safe criterion, not only of means, but of theology. By this criterion, Finney's message and means were "wise."

The Technique of Revival

Finney's adjustment of Calvinistic evangelistic method was consistent with his adjustment of its message. Calvinism's main problem was that "there is no philosophical connection between means and ends in the conversion of sinners." Calvinists continued to insist that the connections were made by God, not man, and what applied to individual sinners also applied to groups. The "new measures" which Finney developed through experience and "laws of the mind" included: (1) direct, exciting, colloquial preaching; (2) four-day protracted meetings given over to preaching, prayer, and counsel with those convicted of sin and anxious to be saved from sunrise to midnight, with all other business in town closed down; (3) anxious seats at public meetings for the convicted who could be singled out for special attention and prayer; (4) public prayer for the conversion of individuals by name; (5) demand for immediate decision; (6) special meetings for the anxious; (6) publicity by handbills; (7) bands of trained personal workers; (7) modern music; and (8) invitation by all resident clergy to hold a revival and a pledge of their cooperation.

Finney refined or created the techniques for staging revivals that became the stock in trade of Protestantism throughout the century. He provided the model for a new form of specialized minister, the professional mass evangelist, who became the norm against which American parish clergy were afterward evaluated. His *Lectures on Rivivals of Religion* became the standard text on the subject for the balance of the century. Finney took the mystery out of mass conversion. It "is not a miracle, nor dependent on a miracle in any sense. It is a purely philosophic result of the right use of the constituted means."[5] After Finney, revivals became a conventional mainstay of the Protestant churches for maintaining vitality and growth.

Finney Measured by the Protestant Adventure

Because Finney was an archetype of the American experience, he provides an accurate sample of how the Protestant adventure was faring through the first two-thirds of the nineteenth century. The "disinterested benevolence" at the heart of the revival experience forged an inevitable link between the reformation of the individual and reformation of society. The glory of God was defined so as to include reform of the world. This kept the two aspects of the original Genevan heritage intact. Only now, the churches were disestablished so that the enforcing of the public side of the adventure would need to find another vehicle than the authority of a theocratic government. In keeping with the theological emphasis on human ability to respond, Protestants formed voluntary societies to implement each of the aspects of the covenant that colonial state governments used to enforce, creating a separate society for each issue. Perhaps most typical were the sabbatarian and temperance associations. Finney was the first to combine a revival with temperance. There were tract, Bible, missionary, and Sabbath-school societies. They were mostly expressions of Protestant morality. The conviction was that if Protestant morality could be imposed on the public at large by suasion, the kingdom of God would come, and soon. Finney spoke for most evangelical clergy in the *Lectures on Revivals*: "If the church will do her duty, the millennium may come in this country in three years."[6]

Finney's ethical instruction showed what duty inner-worldly asceticism called for in his day. The systemic arrangements forged in the Revolution called for no adjustment. But Finney had doubts about the way business was conducted. He was perfectly clear that pursuit of wealth, ostentation, and the profit motive were contrary to disinterested benevolence. He would have prevented all borrowing— but here he only addressed the issue of consumer borrowing. He made no distinction between borrowing capital for production in contrast to consumption. He warned businessmen not to use their profits to enlarge their capital and their businesses. But when asked whether faithful converts should liquidate their capital and give the money to the mission of the churches, he warned against that.

In other words, Finney gave no systematic ethical directions to Protestants caught in the risky adventure of a business world where maximizing profit and growth were the rule. He continued the tradition of just price, and so forth, but gave no instruction to people in particular trades, as had Puritan divines like Baxter. He made no use of the tradition of "calling." In fact he reversed the direction taken by Calvin. One's station in life in terms of affluence was fated. A poor man, if he is a Christian, will be "submissive and happy in his poverty," uncomplaining and unenvious of those who are appointed to grander stations in life. Thus Finney condemned the self-interest and upward mobility that enlightenment economics was declaring belonged to natural law. The "invisible hand" of Adam Smith's *Wealth of Nations*, published in 1776 between Great Awakenings, suggested that an invisible mechanism in the market transformed self-interest into disinterested benevolence. For Finney, only conversion could bring off that transformation.

So Finney put himself and his converts into tension with the world. The difference between Finney and the classic form of inner-worldly asceticism was that with Finney, the tension would be resolved in this world, not in the next. In the last analysis Finney felt that the economic world could be reformed in time for the millennium. "The Christians would soon do the business of the world," if they acted out disinterested benevolence. There was nothing about *laissez faire* capitalism as a system that could prevent reformation by the converted if they did their duty. Perhaps it is significant that there was no voluntary society for the reformation of business.

There was a society for the abolition of slavery. Since the Protestant adventure in America was about to founder on this issue, it is worth our special attention. Finney had been closely related to the abolition movement. His disciples, especially Theodore Weld, were deeply committed to it and tried to get him to combine his revivals with recruitment for the abolition movement. Finney's theory of revivals forbade giving conversion and abolition anything like equal billing. A crucial condition for making revivals work was to keep the public mind focused on a single point—the need to decide for God. Any other subject would distract attention and kill the enterprise. "I did not turn aside to make it (abolition) a hobby or divert the attention of the people from the work of converting souls." Finney had no doubt that slavery was sin, but he told the young abolitionist seminary students at Oberlin, "...that we would accomplish the abolition work much sooner by promoting revivals..." He was convinced that if the church insisted on making abolition an issue ahead of conversion, no Christian response could be expected.

Finney was perfectly clear at this point in the American Protestant experience, that it was of primary importance to make Americans Christian before making America Christian. But the culture had captured Finney to some extent already. Although he was clearly against slavery, abolition did not mean for him equality for blacks. Finney seated blacks and whites separately in his church in New York City and at Oberlin.

Finney saw that in its unconverted state of prejudice, the Protestant church could not handle the issue of slavery.

Methodists in 1804 and 1816, and Presbyterians in 1818, had admitted officially that the subject of slavery was beyond their capacity to resolve, and that the issue would lead to "destructive consequences." In this situation, "Fateful limitations in the search for a Christian America were painfully disclosed."[7]

Other Americans took the issue out of the gradualists hands. Ironically, some of the most influential were Finney's own disciples and supporters. Weld, a Finney convert, and the Tappan brothers, his financial backers, helped make the abolition movement a national evangelical crusade instead of the despised inconvenience it had been before 1840. In spite of Finney, revivalism and abolition eventually combined at Oberlin where Finney was first a professor, and then president. Oberlin became a center of the abolition movement, and many of the techniques associated with revivalism served abolitionism as well.

Hints of Collapse

In some sense the subjects of the Second Great Awakening carried on the Protestant adventure better than its leaders. On the other hand, other subjects of the same Awakening, even while caught up in the experience of it, refused to put ascetic commitment first and instead let the world dictate the shape of their discipleship. For them it was clearly a case of American culture taking precedence over the Protestant adventure. Blacks, in the majority in the South, would have overwhelmed the culture familiar to their white Protestant masters. This, more than economic considerations, led to the collapse of the Protestant adventure there. Whenever either reform of persons or of world is rejected by Protestants, the adventure collapses. In rejecting the abolition movement, southern churches rejected reform of the world.

Taking stock, we see that the Second Great Awakening showed inner-worldly asceticism alive and militant in the first third of the nineteenth century, as the Calvinist heritage was shaped to American experience. The resulting indigenous theology included both an intense inner experience in continuity with the contemplative, mystical tradition of the middle ages and its companion thrust to reform the world according to the will of a sovereign God. The American world seemed so amenable to evangelical reform, it verged on becoming the kingdom of God—except for the issue of slavery. That issue showed that when forced to choose, American Protestants felt a greater commitment to certain aspects of their culture than to the classic Protestant adventure. Indeed, the world proved itself as risky a place for Protestants as Bunyan in *Pilgrims Progress* had assumed. But slavery aside, Protestants had probably never been so optimistic about the world. Not only was the world on the verge of becoming the kingdom of God, but individuals also seemed to offer no insurmountable obstacle to complete sanctification.

But there was also the hint of a suggestion that revivalism might not be so completely effective with persons as the Great Awakenings pretended. The new theology had given persons free reign over their own destinies, and in principle, if one was free to enter the Protestant adventure, one was just as free to leave; many revival converts did just that. A critic of Finney in 1835 observed that" . . . numerous converts of the new measures have been in most cases like the morning cloud and the early dew. In some places, not a half, a fifth, or even a tenth part of them remain."[8] In 1836 Finney himself admitted that most of his own converts were "a disgrace to religion" because of their "low standard of piety."

The area where Finney had his conversion experience and hammered out the new measures, western New York, was the scene of so many revivals that it soon became immune to the appeal of evangelical religion and earned the name "the burned over district." Did this in part stimulate the invention of an alternative religion? Was one inhabitant of the area so fed up with the flurry and wrangling of reviving Protestants, that he was driven to invent his own religion? Joseph Smith published *The Book of Mormon* in Palmyra in 1830.[9]

In an attempt to come to terms with the limitations of the revival experience, Finney embraced perfectionism. "My stay at every place was too short to accomplish much in the work of leading converts to manhood in religion. The same is true of my brethren who have been evangelists." This was in 1836. In 1839 he explained further, "I was fully convinced that converts would die—that the standard of piety would never be elevated—that revivals would become more and more superficial and finally cease unless something effectual was done to elevate the standard of holiness in the church." To provide a higher standard of piety he advocated a second blessing, baptism of the Holy Spirit which would move a convert to a stage of sanctification beyond the ordinary revival experience. This would lead to the perfection of which all were capable under Finney's doctrine of "ability equal to obligation." The truly sanctified "habitually live without sin and fall into sin only at intervals so few and far between that, in strong language, it may be said in truth they do not sin."

This solution amounted in effect to one more application of the revival experience. What was missing was the tightly knit, covenant community of the colonial churches before disestablishment. They had provided the context necessary for stability and growth among converts. Covenanted congregations had encouraged and enforced a standard of piety that distinguished the convert from others by more than a declared intention to carry out disinterested benevolence. And all the sanctions of society stood behind the convert.

The Second Awakening created a situation in which the adventuring Protestant was isolated in a relatively indifferent culture no longer organized around discipleship, but committed instead to progressive individualism. A devotee of the marketplace does not need a supportive community when "he intends only his own gain . . . pursuing his own interest." Without such community support, a convert is almost bound to default even when he or she intends "disinterested benevolence." The failure of revivalism to build discipling communities would prove the truth of Wesley's observation that, "Christianity is essentially a social religion; to turn it into a solitary religion is indeed to destroy it."[10]

·4·

The Third Awakening (1875–1915)

The Private and Public Parties of the Gilded Age

If an awakening is defined as the response of the church to a crisis in the culture at large, then the last quarter of the last century threw America as a whole into a crisis as fateful as any in the American experience.[1] It was the most fateful crisis of all for the Protestant adventure because its response to that crisis was collapse. Consensus among Protestants about what their adventure entailed and how to pursue it evaporated—and ever since the collapse, American protestants have been nurturing one another into misadventures: pale, partial, truncated, grotesque versions of the real thing. Only unflinching acceptance of this fact can set the stage for recovery of the Protestant adventure and of the Protestant identity that goes with it.

Historians often refer to the last quarter of the last century as the Gilded Age. That term may capture the experience of the churches even better than the term "awakening." It was an awakening but not in the sense of reappropriating the heritage of the Protestant adventure to meet the new turn of events in a faithful way. Instead it was an awakening to another adventure, to the adventure of the middle-class scramble for quick riches. Instead of resisting the emergence of the Gilded Age, the churches themselves helped to create it.

Protestants were bound to have had a part in preparing for the Gilded Age because they were the most powerful influence in the culture in the middle third of the century. "In . . . many ways, the middle third of the nineteenth century was more of a 'Protestant Age' than was the colonial period with its established churches,"[2] as church influence was felt most dramatically in the pressure that surrounded the antislavery and proslavery movements. The Protestant pressure for and against slavery which escalated after 1830 contributed significantly to the causes of the Civil War. But other pressures were building during that same period which subverted inner-worldly asceticism in an even more fundamental fashion than resistance to Christian social responsibility that accompanied the slavery and segregation issues.

The Triumph of Clerical Economics

Notice had been served on Protestant asceticism in the revolutionary period with the publication of Adam Smith's *Wealth of Nations*. Cultural heroes like Ben Franklin emerged as the embodiment of the spirit of capitalism. In effect, the collapse in England of the Puritan adventure was catching up with their children's children in the new world. Smith's theory of self-interested economic motives described a habit that Englishmen had been forming for a hundred years; by the time Adam Smith formulated the theory to justify the practice, the practice was thoroughly engrained. ". . . spontaneous, doctrineless individualism . . . became the rule of English public life a century before the philosophy of it was propounded by Adam Smith . . ."[3]

From the Puritan period to the present, American clergy have denounced the perils of materialism and worldliness. The paradox of Puritan inner-worldly asceticism is that, given the natural potential of the land they settled, their patterns of work done to the glory of God, quickly resulted in prosperity. In New England "there were complaints of a peculiarly calculating sort of profitseeking . . . as early as

1632." There is little doubt that clergy devoted to the principle of worldly vocation as work done as unto God and devotees of avarice existed together from the beginning, and that clergy were supporting economic virtues. But the vast majority of colonial clergy knew the difference between a Puritan who kept the covenant and devotees of avarice.

Franklin promoted devotion to avarice beyond anything available in seventeenth-century America. The following passage catches the spirit of his advice. It is the earliest description in America of the work-a-holic.

> The most trifling actions that affect a man's credit are to be regarded. The sound of your hammer at five in the morning, or eight at night, heard by a creditor, makes him easy six months longer; but if he sees you at a billiard table, or hears your voice at a tavern, when you should be at work, he sends for his money the next day; demands it, before he can receive it, in a lump.[4]

Every ascetic American Protestant would have known the difference between the image Franklin was building and inner-worldly asceticism. Franklin's was just plain worldly asceticism.

During the period of industrial expansion, from the 1830s on, the living standards of every American rose. In this period American clergy were increasingly influenced in their interpretation of the meaning of piety, work, money, and social responsibility by economic theorists like Adam Smith, rather than the biblical theological tradition that had shaped the Puritan experience. The major shift in theological perspective concerning history and the work world was the assumption of "clerical economics"—the idea that natural law in economics and the revealed religion of the biblical tradition do not contradict each other. Protestant clergy from Edwards to Finney had agreed that God's Providence and natural law were directly related, but the world of natural law and economics could be viewed realistically only within the context of the whole of Protestant history. Thus, the God revealed through the medium of the Bible could and did stand in judgment of the economic and social systems devised by human beings.

The remarkable shift in perspective that occurred in "clerical economics" made it possible for increasingly prosperous middle-class church members and their clergy to congratulate themselves on the prosperity that attended their work because God was rewarding them for their "ascetic" work habits. While Finney remained very much aware of the danger of wealth to Protestants in the 1830s, parish clergy were increasingly reversing this traditional Protestant estimate of the market place.

In 1836 the Reverend Thomas P. Hunt wrote in *The Book of Wealth*, "No man can be obedient to God's will...without becoming wealthy." Francis Wayland, president of Brown, authored in 1837 the most popular American text on economics. It sold fifty thousand copies by 1867, and was in continuous print until 1875.[5] His influence amounted to pastoral care among Protestants. In 1835 he wrote in a popular text on ethics, "God intends that man should grow rich."

Poverty Reappraised

When wealth becomes the mark of the favorites of God, the status of the poor must be redefined. A similar redefinition occurred in England when the Puritan version of the Protestant adventure collapsed there, just as a similar adjustment in theology occurred in both settings. "A society which reverences the attainment of riches as the supreme felicity will naturally be disposed to regard the poor as damned in the next world, if only to justify itself for making their life a hell in this."[6] Instead of being the favorites of God and the monitors of true piety, possibly the incognito Christ, the poor became a necessary element in the motivation of the economic system. As in the English Puritan development, Puritanism in America led eventually to another triumph of "economic virtue."

Jonathan Wainwright was rector of Boston's Trinity Church when, in 1835, he preached on the text commonly used to hedge traditional responsibility, "The poor shall never cease out of the land" (Deut. 15:11). In his sermon Wainwright said, "The unequal distribution of wealth we believe to be not only an unalterable consequence of the nature of man, and the state of being in which he is placed, but also the only system by which his happiness and improvement can be promoted in this state of being." He also warned against indiscriminate help for the poor, skipping over the rest of his text which reads, "therefore I command you to open wide your hand to your brother, to the needy, and to the poor"! When the obligation to the poor is removed, an absolute right to property is safe, therefore Wainwright concluded, "Once touch the rights of property . . . and you immediately stop enterprise."

In the middle third of the century, Protestant clergy were helping prepare for the collapse of their grand adventure. "In the twilight years between the old merchant or commercial economy, and the beginnings of the new industrial one, the middle classes passed an informal but binding new social contract, and did so with benefit of clergy."[7]

Advancing Industrial Revolution

With clerical economics supporting unrestrained free enterprise, the churches of the Gilded Age were completely unprepared to cope with the advanced Industrial Revolution when it hit. Distracted by revival concentration on an ever more isolated experience of conversion, and compromised by the shift in economic perspective, the churches got out of the habit of apprising the faithful of the risks of being Protestant, and lost the skills to direct people in the face of those risks. To adjust the metaphor—"whom the gods destroy, they first distract." "Surprise has sometimes been expressed that the Church should not have been more effective in giving inspiration during the 'Industrial Revolution'. It did not give it, because it did not possess it."[8]

> The church born among the poor and developed for their passion and solace was coming to despise the outcasts. The church born to be suspicious of riches licensed

unregulated gain. The Protestant churches, shaped in a colonial America which had fostered commonwealth concepts, chartered individualism. A tradition which had exalted persons over property, converted and justified absolute rights to property on the part of the industrious. The ideal of organismic community was overshadowed by a religion which largely accepted the laissez-faire competitive enterprise system.[9]

Arthur M. Schlesinger, Sr., called 1875–1900 "A critical period in American religion." For the Protestant adventure in America, it was *the* critical period.[10] The economic system took a quantum jump. Railroads tied newly discovered resources together with newly discovered manufacturing skills, steam supplying the power everywhere. An agricultural nation became a manufacturing nation. The factory system and urban overcrowding took over. Economic power concentrated itself in the hands of a relatively few masterful entrepreneurs, and working people became economic units in a vast impersonal system. Face to face economic transaction became the exception, rather than the rule.

If the churches were not ready, individual Protestants were. Now the economic virtues could be made to pay off in an unprecedented way. Four thousand millionaires arose in America before the Gilded Age was over. How did Protestants respond to this new wealth? By and large they embraced it as though it represented the coming of the kingdom. After the Civil War, America seemed weary of its ascetic heritage. "Everywhere was a welling-up of primitive pagan desires after long repressions—to grow rich, to grasp power, to be strong and masterful and lay the world at its feet. Freedom and opportunity, to acquire, to possess, to enjoy—for that it would sell its soul."[11] It was a time somewhat like post-Restoration England when the Puritan form of the Protestant adventure collapsed there.

Prominent clergy helped justify the change in mood by transforming traditional symbols. Russell Conwell and Henry Ward Beecher became national figures by legitimizing the shift away from inner-worldly asceticism to a "decorous worldliness." Conwell was a businessman turned clergy. He produced a sermon-lecture that became the most popular lecture ever. Conwell estimated that he delivered it six thousand times for a total honorarium of eight million dollars.[12] He titled it "Acres of Diamonds."

The theme of the lecture published in 1890 was that anybody could get rich if they took advantage of their opportunities and realized that it was God's will that they should. Typical passages were: "...unless some of you get richer for what I am saying tonight, my time is wasted." "I say you ought to get rich and it is your duty to get rich." "...ninety-eight out of one hundred of the rich men in America are honest. That is why they are rich." Along with the sanctification of wealth came the inevitable downgrading of the poor.

> I won't give in but what I sympathize with the poor, but the number of the poor who are to be sympathized with is very small. To sympathize with a man whom God has punished for his sins, thus to help when God would still continue a just punishment, is to do wrong, no doubt about it...[13]

Conwell preached in Philadelphia. Meanwhile, in Brooklyn, Henry Ward Beecher (1818–87), the greatest pulpit orator of his day, was offering similar advice, counseling the poor to be content with their lot while he supplemented his income doing commercials for Pear's Soap, and carried around pocketfuls of uncut gems. "It is said that a dollar a day is not enough for a wife and five or six children...is not a dollar a day enough to buy bread with? Water costs nothing; and a man who cannot live on bread is not fit to live."[14] Beecher's callousness stemmed from his conviction about the root of poverty.

> There may be reasons of poverty which do not involve wrong; but looking comprehensively through city and town and village and country, the general truth will stand, that no man in this land suffers from poverty unless it be more than his fault—unless it be his sin.[15]

People like Beecher knew they were teaching no New Testament view of riches, but they surmounted the difficulties. "... we are not to stand and inveigh against riches, and (no doubt with the story of Jesus and the rich young ruler in mind) we are not to warn young men against becoming, or desiring to become, rich." Episcopalian Bishop Lawrence acknowledged that the Bible teaches the danger of wealth to morality, but countered, "In the long run, it is only to the men of morality that wealth comes.... Godliness is in league with riches."[16] If the preachers themselves were aware that they were not offering a biblical message, where did that message originate?

The Gospel of Wealth

The new message came from the surrounding culture through essays written by millionaires like Andrew Carnegie about "the true Gospel concerning Wealth."[17] The "Captain of Industry" served as the culture's model of the Christian person. Tenets of the gospel of Christian manhood were that the economic world is ruled by a natural aristocracy who have proved their right to govern by their rise to the top of the economic pyramid. The state, being run by inferiors, should confine itself to a police function and not interfere in economic matters. The sense of stewardship of the wealthy and their native abilities make them best qualified to distribute the wealth to the needy and less able. In Carnegie's own version of the gospel, the rich were to distribute all their wealth before they died lest unworthy men come to control it. (However, this variation on the gospel of wealth was not widely shared.) What was widely accepted was the idea that the individual must be granted maximum freedom to rise to wealth; poverty and wealth were thought to be distributed justly by the system. This was the gospel that displaced the Protestant one. It got powerful "scientific" support from Social Darwinism, and became the reigning social philosophy of the Gilded Age.

By adopting the gospel of wealth, the vast majority of Protestants defaulted on their Adventure, making the pursuit of wealth the aim of life and reneging on their social responsibility. Protestants dropped the goal of a reformed society to match reformed individuals. They condemned social reform in the economic realm as inconsistent with individual freedom, now absolutized in the revised version of the gospel.

How could such capitulation to the world have happened? The Puritan vision of America as God's new chosen race led eventually to the conclusion after the Second Great Awakening that the churches were appointed by God to Christianize America. The idea of a Christian civilization became so powerful that American civilization and American national history itself began to be equated with Christianity. It was an easy next step for that civilization to come to dictate the meaning of being Christian. That step was taken in the Gilded Age.

> In the earlier period, the priority of the religious vision was strongly and widely maintained; it was Christianity *and* civilization, Christianity as the best part of civilization, and its hope. In the latter part of the century, however, in most cases unconsciously, much of the real focus had shifted to the civilization itself, with Christianity and the churches finding their significance in relation to it.[18]

Poor Richard had been baptized and he took over. Protestants were defeated by their own success. Convinced that they had set the tone for culture, culture set the tone for Protestantism from then on. The special sense of national election which English colonists had brought with them gave to America the sense of being a "nation with the soul of a church."

There was some ambivalence toward this new national status, which arose as the human price exacted for industrial advance became more apparent. To staff the factories and mines, waves of non-English, non-Protestant workers came to America. Especially in the cities where they congregated, they brought a cultural ethos "foreign" to Anglo-Saxon

America. The periodic, arbitrary deprivations of industrial capitalism led to massive worker discontent, and unions began to have some success in organizing labor for a larger, more secure share of the benefits of industrial advance. According to the clerical economics, the labor share was fixed by natural (and divine) law so that strikes for a larger share were contrary to God and nature, but workers struck in spite of this conventional wisdom. The resulting conflict did not fit the vision of Christian America, nor did the crowding and the public immorality of burgeoning cities. The unfortunate changes that the industrial revolution brought to American culture called for an adjustment in evangelical vision of the last days.

The Private Party

From the beginning most American churches had operated with a postmillennial view of the climax of history. By gaining more and more control of the morality of the culture, Protestants had hoped to inaugurate the millennium, a thousand year reign of Christ on earth which would completely embody the kingdom of God. Divine judgment and separation to heaven and hell would follow. As the course of American history veered away from millennial fulfillment, some forms of popular theology shifted ground and began to maintain that the return of Christ and the final judgment would take place before, "pre", the millennium—hence the name premillennialism."

From either a postmillennial or a premillennial perspective, the church and the Christian had no obligation to change the world. A postmillennialist, like Henry Ward Beecher, claimed that it was God's natural law for society to weed out undeserving persons through the process of natural selection. The kingdom would evolve through a natural process of moral and racial purification. A premillennialist, like Dwight L. Moody, left the reformation of the world to the divine intervention of God, who would deal with it at the End. Either way, the church was responsible to change only individuals, but not the world in which they lived.

This new estimate of the American world was seldom carried out with consistency. On the supposition that the world is so far gone as to be beyond the possibility of redemptive change, then the Christian should withdraw from sharing its values to avoid contamination. The major contact with such an evil world ought to take the form of evangelism and for the rest a highly cautious participation. Here the ambiguity took over. While revising their estimate of the world for purposes of social change, most Protestants continued to embrace the clerical economics of laissez faire in their work-a-day lives. The new world of industrial America was too evil to change, but too good to miss.

By this response Protestants lost touch with the essence of the tradition of inner-worldly asceticism and the Protestant adventure which it entailed. What continued was the revival experience. But now that experience no longer linked converts with the world in a responsible reforming fashion. The response of the churches to the Gilded Age was so partial and truncated, that it no longer deserved to be called Protestant in the sense of the great adventure. What appeared in the Gilded Age was party Protestantism, using "party" in the sense of a partial view represented by one group in conflict with another. Private-party Protestantism continued only the individualistic side of the gospel of inner-worldly asceticism, dropping the social side, except as it claimed that converted individuals could make a significant difference to the morality of the world. Efforts on behalf of prohibition and sabbatarianism continued, but concern for economic reform evaporated in complete capitulation to the gospel of wealth of the Gilded Age.

Dwight L. Moody, Private Party Champion

The most representative figure of the private party during the Third Awakening was Dwight L. Moody, a former shoe salesman and Sunday School organizer. He was *the* evangelist of the Third Awakening, using with flair all of the measures which Finney and his contemporaries had devised and an intervening generation of revivalists had honed. Until the Gilded Age, evangelists tended to be adventurous, experimental, ahead of their times. Moody and his successors were behind their times helping nostalgic private-party Protestants to resist change with the methods and message of a past generation. Moody's career began in 1872 with a successful crusade in England. His greatest years as a mass evangelist were 1873–1883. He died in 1899. It is striking that neither of the two main figures of the Second and Third Awakening had theological educations; Moody was educated through the seventh grade. That background gave him little chance to be aware either of the Protestant tradition, or of the cultural forces of which he was a pawn. Finney had made revivalism a profession; Moody made it big business.[19]

Moody's views offer a fair summary of the private party's response to this critical period in American history. As a revivalist, he represented the continuation of the dependence of the churches on evangelism as the key to their mission. Like Finney, he resented any distraction from the main business of winning souls, for example, woman suffrage was a "master stroke of the devil." Serious concern for a theological understanding of conversion evaporated. In response to a question about his theology, Moody once said, "My theology! I didn't know I had any. I wish you would tell me what my theology is." On another occasion he said, "I am an Armenian up to the Cross; after the Cross, a Calvinist."

The essence of Moody's theology was a shift from the Genevan, Puritan God of awesome judgment to a loving, friendly Christ who would be a comforting companion in everyday life. The conversion experience itself was greatly simplified. The essence of decision was to believe that Christ had died for one's sins—in return one was guaranteed eternal life. Moody offered a "second blessing" which would completely sanctify one for service. The second blessing of the Spirit was "so that they shall have the power." Conviction of sin preparatory to decision came in response to dwelling on the details of the crucifixion as the source of a sense of guilt, rather than on the threat of hell, as had been the custom since the Great Awakening.

A major benefit of conversion was economic success, especially for the poor. "I don't see how a man can follow Christ and not be successful." If one did not become successful, that person had probably not been truly converted. "There are a great many professing Christians who never get on intimate terms with God and so they never amount to much." During a depression in New York City in 1876, with fifty thousand unemployed, he explained that it was because "sufferers have been lost from the Shepherd's care." The economic system was not to blame and of course needed no reformation. By appealing to the return of Christ, Moody taught that the world could not be reformed. "I look upon this world as a wrecked vessel, God has given me a lifeboat and said to me, 'Moody, save all you can!'"

Moody used his premillennialism to counter criticism of his revivals and of his opposition to social action. While pessimistic about reforming the world because it would be left behind at the return of Christ, he had confidence that the system worked for the Christian who wished to rise. "They will make room for you." This confidence in an evil but economically just world made Moody and the private party he represented a militant foe of the labor movement. It was permissible to rise via the economic virtues, but not by strike, boycotts, and agitation.

Although Moody was the most skilled engineer of revival in the evangelistic tradition, records kept at the time showed that he actually did not touch the working classes, nor the poor and unchurched of the cities where he held campaigns. He recycled church members and converts of former campaigns. In other words, Moody and the party he represented could not relate to the non-Anglo-Saxon newcomers to America who were the laborers of the industrial revolution. Moody knew that this was the major challenge to Protestant America. He founded Moody Bible Institute in answer to what he called "the greatest subject before the people today" which was, "what should be done with the working man?"

His only answer was to convert him to the private party. "A heart that is right with God and man seldom constitutes a social problem, and by seeking first the kingdom of God and His righteousness, nine-tenths of social betterment is effected by the convert himself and the other tenth by Christian sympathy." Moody's failure to touch the working class in America was typical of Protestantism in the Gilded Age. Protestantism in America would more and more be confined to a special stratum within the population. The Third Awakening showed Protestantism to be well on its way to a second disestablishment.

In substituting soul-winning for reform, Moody was responding to the challenge of industrialization, urbanization, and immigration. In addition, the crisis in American culture of the critical period included the intellectual challenges of Darwinian evolution and historical criticism of the Bible. Moody was typical of the private party in his implicit acceptance of the social side of Darwinism and his explicit rejection of its biological side. Biological evolution was rejected because it contradicted the account of creation in Genesis, but the struggle for survival was accepted as the divine model for society. In effect Moody promised that conversion would make a Christian the most fit in that worldly struggle. A world locked in the struggle to survive suited the premillennial view of the End. But biological evolution did not fit a literal interpretation of the Bible, so that was rejected. The major conflict with the new learning of both Darwinism and historical criticism was that it challenged the view of the Bible as literally inerrant—God's final word on any subject it raised. The argument over slavery had made this view of the Bible a comfort to the southern slave owner. Since the Bible assumed the presence of the institution of slavery, slave holding must be compatible with true Christianity. Likewise the Bible knew nothing of the Industrial Revolution, unions, and collective bargaining, so they were outside the bounds of Christian concern. By refusing to allow God to speak a further, clarifying word to the new situation of industrialization and its attendant tragedies, private-party Protestants turned Christianity into a religion that condoned the worst features of the Gilded Age.

This view of the Bible not only acted as a barrier to social change, it also subverted intellectual growth. Historical study of the Bible discovered it to be a library of books representative of many different viewpoints spread over a vast range of time and historical circumstances. An historical view of the formation of the Bible and of the formation of each book within it helped to explain the obvious variety of viewpoints and what beforehand had seemed like contradiction. There were contradictions only if one assumed a single divine system of doctrine unencumbered by a variety of authors and circumstances. Historical criticism helped to explain "contradictions" by calling attention to the historical character of Scripture. So-called contradictions were actually the product of a rigid doctrinal mold which Protestant scholasticism had clamped onto the Bible in ignorance of its true historical character. Typical of his party, Moody simply refused to deal with the contradictions that his view of the Bible created. If he did not understand a contradictory passage and could not explain it, he still believed it. In a conversation with George Adam Smith, one of the leading biblical scholars of the time, Moody rejected higher criticism simply because it was creating division in the church and hindering the work of revivals and evangelism.[20] Although the private party eventually generated a much more complex and learned response to historical criticism,[21] Moody fairly represented what this wing of American Protestantism concluded about the Bible—and what most Protestants continue to believe today.

Gargoyle Christians

The private party response to the crisis of the Gilded Age produced grotesque Christians from the point of view of the great Protestant tradition of inner-worldly asceticism. It left converts wracked between the pull of a conversion experience with the promise of complete sanctification, and uncritical acceptance of a world dominated by a careless economic system on whose terms they had to confirm their salvation. It is no wonder that many who pursued this schizoid existence wound up somewhat misshapen compared to a classic portrait of the Protestant adventure.

One such gargoyle on the Protestant facade in the Gilded Age was Daniel Drew. "There was Uncle Dan'l Drew, thin as a dried herring, yet a builder of churches and founder of Drew Theological Seminary, who pilfered and cheated his way to wealth with tobacco juice drooling from his mouth...Daniel Drew was a shyster cattle drover, whose arid emotions found outlet in periodic conversions and backslidings, and who got on in this vale of tears by salting his cattle and increasing his and the Lord's wealth with every pound of water in their bellies—from which cleverness is said to have come the Wall-Street phrase, 'stockwatering.'"[22] It is easy to be censorious until one realizes that the gospel of wealth of the private party in the Gilded Age actually encouraged this inconsistent and self-contradictory form of religion. Watergate is its natural heir.

The Public Party

Not all American Protestants during the Gilded Age were private-party Christians. The social-gospel movement, a group of socially aware clergy and seminary professors, incorporated a more positive response to biblical scholarship and parts of Social Darwinism into a new biblical theology at the turn of the century. Like Henry Ward Beecher, social-gospel leaders were postmillennialists who believed that America might be "almost" Christianized. Unlike Beecher, they had a social conscience concerning the plight of the poor and oppressed, especially women and children, in the interim before the kingdom of God was realized in concrete form in America.

The social-gospel men, or public-party Protestants, were lineal descendants of Finney in that they considered both change in individuals and change in society important to the task of the church to usher in the coming kingdom. The "if" clause in their sense of social responsibility, was that "if" the church could convert uncivilized members of the American nation to the standards of conduct evident in the love and peace seen in the Christian family, then the kingdom would come. Although public party leaders acknowledged a need for limited legislation in the interest of social justice for non-Anglo-Saxons, like Finney, they still thought individual change was the key to social change. They continued to renew the impulse of the Second Awakening to Christianize America.

Washington Gladden, Public Party Founder

Washington Gladden (1836–1918) is considered the father and perhaps the most representative figure of the public party.[23] As an adolescent he was not able to manage the mystical experience which revival Protestantism held up as the ideal. Any theology that called for such an experience had no appeal for him. The effects of the antislavery movement in his home church in Oswego, New York, appealed to him, and he chose the ministry. After Williams College and tutoring in theology, he accepted ordination in the Congregational church in 1860. Like Moody and Finney, Gladden was ordained without benefit of a formal theological education. Three books by Gladden combining liberal theology with social concern were widely read. His first parish assignment was in Brooklyn. The contrast between life there and his own rural background made a deep impression on him. His service in the Civil War put him in firsthand contact with reconstruction. In 1866 he took a church in a manufacturing town, North Adams, Massachusetts, where imported Chinese laborers gave him his first experience of labor conflict. A talented writer, he next worked for the *Independent* in New York, which deepened his acquaintance with urban problems.

The turning point in his ministry came with his acceptance of the pulpit of the First Congregational Church of Columbus, Ohio, in 1882, where he remained until 1914. That post put him in direct contact with an important labor battle, the Hocking Valley coal strike of 1884. Coal company officials, some of whom belonged to the First Church, broke the union by forcing them back to work under an agreement forbidding union activity. A year later, another strike forced arbitration to the workers' advantage. These experiences led Gladden to strong convictions, effectively expressed, against competition and self-interest as the basis for setting wages. "The doctrine which bases all the relations of employer and employed upon self-interest is a doctrine of the pit; it has been bringing hell to earth in large installments for a good many years." "The labor of the nation is the life of the nation; is that a commodity to be bought in the cheapest market and sold in the dearest?"[24]

In a famous address, "Is It Peace or War?", he argued that labor had a right to use whatever means was necessary, because labor-management relations were in a state of war. That was the most forthright challenge to the assumptions of clerical economics that any Protestant clergyperson had advanced before 1886. As a Christian, Gladden did not advocate war. His alternative was profit-sharing and a reduction of the length of the working day without a reduction in wages. Gladden's realistic analysis of the workers' share in increasing the wealth of the society disclosed that while labor had tripled its production in twenty-five years, it had not increased its share of the benefits. By the last two decades of the century, Gladden was as influential as any Protestant clergyperson in America. During his career he published thirty-six books. He distanced himself from socialism while advocating public ownership of utilities and cooperative management of industry. He maintained that rights to property should be limited by social use.

Gladden's theology made him optimistic in spite of his realistic appreciation of the problems of labor. He exchanged the revivalist experience of conversion and its view of the sinfulness of human beings for the then current doctrine of a nearly perfected human race capable of brotherhood to all men. Since Gladden had not been able to manage the experience which revivalists had called for, he defined conversion to mean that anyone, who so willed, could "change their mind" and reorient their lives to the moral obedience required by God of the converted. No revivalist was needed to midwife such a change. For Gladden this was the natural response to inspiring preaching. Church membership was sufficient evidence of inner change.

The private party accused Gladden of having no theology and made a point of pitting one of its representatives against him. In 1912 Billy Sunday brought a revival campaign to Columbus where Gladden was a pastor. Gladden quietly opposed the coming of the campaign and was sharply critical of it afterward. The vast majority of Protestant ministers arose to Sunday's defense and attacked Gladden.[25] By the end of the Third Awakening, it had become clear that from then on, for American Protestantism, the two components of inner-worldly asceticism were seen as competitive, rather than complementary. Protestantism had largely jettisoned its classic adventure.

The last figure in American history who attempted to represent the whole adventure in a single ministry was a professional evangelist named B. Fay Mills. A friend of Gladden's, he sought to combine the personal conversion of revivalism with commitment to the social gospel. Partly through his superior organizational techniques, he rose to the top of his profession in the five years after 1891. "But it proved impossible to preach both individual repentance and social responsibility from a revival platform. Neither the preachers, nor the church members, wanted or expected it."[26] American Protestantism has not seen anyone attempt that combination since Mills.[27]

The Collapse of the Protestant Adventure

The crises in America which the Third Awakening addressed demonstrated that Protestantism could not respond faithfully to the challenges of a changing world. It could only manage partial responses, each of which lost something essential to the classic Protestant identity. The majority of

Protestants chose the private-party response of personal conversion coupled with social irresponsibility; yet the method of propagating this viewpoint, mass evangelism, proved to be less and less effective in winning new converts to even that brand of Protestantism. The public party became even less influential, and the social gospel went into eclipse with the failure of the idealism of the progressive movement to meet the hard realities of World War I and increased resistance within the business community. The public party had never had a large constituency in the churches. Its concerns were now carried forward mainly by secular advocates so that the protest dimension of Protestantism moved for the most part outside the church where it could be served without the vetoing power of a majority of church members.

When Charles Stelzle, the secretary of the Presbyterian church's department of church and labor, protested "the unnecessary slaughter of workingmen in the Pittsburgh rolling mills," the moderator warned him that he "was killing the goose that lays the golden egg," since so many prominent Presbyterians helped to manage the steel industry. Stelzle was first warned, then his budget cut; he resigned in 1913. The *Presbyterian* welcomed his resignation with, "Mr. Stelzle started out in the service of the Gospel, but his drift and development has been into and along sociology."[28]

One cannot exaggerate the import of the failure of the Third Awakening to meet faithfully the challenge of the modern world. Ever since then, Protestants have had the opportunity to appropriate only part of their heritage. Americans, sensing somehow that Protestantism is in collapse, have gradually assigned it a more and more peripheral role in American life. The supreme tragedy has been that each party was so captured by the world that even the part of classical Protestantism that each preserved was compromised and trivialized.

The Trivialization of Conversion

The private party fell prey to Social Darwinism as the explanation of how the perfect social order of the coming kingdom would occur. Conversion became progressively more disengaged from responsible, social life. It finally retained little of the challenge and genuine personal reorientation conversion represented in the first two awakenings. The decision card that Mills passed out, pledged only that, "I have an honest desire henceforth to lead a Christian life."[29] Many of the people who did sign cards were former converts responding to the invitation to reconsecrate their lives.

Billy Sunday, the last of the innovative evangelists, simply dispensed with inquiry rooms. A handshake replaced all of that. He also did away with the apparatus for counseling convicted sinners. Mostly people smiled as they came forward. To Sunday, conversion meant for many a modest increase in decency. "Multitudes of men live good, honest, upright, moral lives. They will not have much to change to become a Christian." Often his invitations were merely: "Do you believe it's right and manly to be a Christian? Then come on down. If you don't, stay where you are." Sometimes it was: "I want the inspiration of taking the hand of every fellow who says, 'I'm with you for Jesus Christ and for truth.' Come on." The invitation to repentance and regeneration could even be: "Come on down and take my hand against booze, for Jesus Christ, for your flag."[30] (At times Sunday climaxed his sermon by standing on the pulpit and waving the United States flag.)

The Trivialization of Social Change

The public party trivialized its contribution to a similar degree. Although Gladden worked for social reform in the immediate present, he *expected* as a result, in the near future, "the nation in its purposes and policies and ruling aims (would become) essentially Christian." This hope was possible because the social gospel characteristically equated democracy—and the family as democracy in microcosm—with the kingdom of God. Rauschenbush, the theologian of the public party, concluded in 1912 that the only sector of the social order remaining to be Christianized was business. Family, church, school, and politics were already vehicles of the spirit of Christ. The public party was captive to a progressive version of Social Darwinism that led them to believe that their actions made the establishment of the kingdom of God in America possible. The private party replaced the power of God with the instrumentality of the evangelist, while the public party replaced the power of God with the instrumentality of the social reformer.

"The concern for civilization which in the early nineteenth century had been secondary to the religious mission, was now often being put first, with religious mission as a means to the end of the Christianization of civilization. The priorities had subtly been reversed; men were being exhorted to be religious for the sake of civilization. Often unconsciously, an idealized Americanism had become the real center of interest for many Christians."[31]

The most stunning incongruity of that commitment to American civilization was almost complete disregard for the fate of native Americans and American blacks, who because they did not share the manners and mores of that civilization, were systematically excluded from its benefits and from participation in its mainstream life. While the social gospel flowered, blacks were being disenfranchised in the South and subjected to Jim Crowism everywhere. The social-gospel leader Lyman Abbott considered it a contribution to "civilization" that native Americans were relieved of their land and confined to unproductive tracts of land for which latecomer Americans had no use. This was accomplished by a series of broken treaties interpreted as necessary to hasten the coming kingdom, that must surely stand as unique in the history of the idea of covenant and contract. Though the public party acted as conscience and custodian for the rights of God's people, vast segments of that people went uncared for.

Each party compromised even its strong points; its weak points were abysmally inadequate. The private lives of public-party types were left to the mercy of a vague "enthusiasm for humanity" because they believed that the moral nature of mankind had evolved to near perfection just as surely as the physical order of the universe had evolved to its highest and best form in the nineteenth century. And as for the private party, they delivered their converts to a world locked in a jungle struggle to weed out the unfit and charged them to do what was required to survive. "Christians were ... placed in the novel situation of having to explain away the very classes of people among whom they conceived the Church to have been born, and for whom the Gospel had been proclaimed: the poor, the outcast, the downtrodden, the overlooked, the materially hopeless of the world."[32]

Protestantism had thought to possess American civilization for the greater glory of its God. Instead, American civilization cast a spell on Protestantism that left it halt and half-blind.

·5·

The Aftermath of the Third Awakening

The aftermath of the breakdown of Protestantism in America is the story of fruitless controversy, the refining of each party's distortions, and a progressive disestablishment of Protestantism as the formative influence in the culture. World War I and the subsequent scuttling of the idealism of the League of Nations led to frustration and disillusionment in the public party. The twenties saw a return to the prosperity that the private party's public policy advocated. But that prosperity did not enhance the life of the churches. Instead, the years of increasing prosperity saw a decline in church attendance and giving, with contributions to missions peaking in 1921 and declining steadily thereafter. Spiritual depression had set in by the mid-twenties, so that when the economic depression came, there was no religious response. Protestants were no longer reading the course of America's experience in terms of interaction with Providence; the fate of the nation was thought to rest in other hands. Then and thereafter, when America faced economic crisis, it would turn to politicians and scientific economists: the answer to the crash of 1929 was the New Deal, a wholly secular remedy.

Neo-orthodoxy and the Public Party

In 1935 the public party showed signs of life in the form of a critique of its own theology and program. That critique was a search for "realism." It was preceded by a deep and pervasive sense that American Christianity had been domesticated by, and made captive to, American culture. Perhaps the clearest call to Protestants to withdraw from this worldly captivity came in a slim volume of three essays entitled, *The Church Against the World.*[1] The authors were H. Richard Niebuhr, Wilhelm Pauck, and Francis R. Miller. Much of what is conveyed in this survey of the situation of American Protestants was movingly expressed there over forty years ago. In answer to the question "Is America Christian?", Miller replied:

> The plain fact is that the domestication of the Protestant community in the United States within the framework of the national culture has progressed as far as in any western land. The degradation of the American Protestant church is as complete as the degradation of any other national Protestant church ... a process which began with a culture molded by religious faith has ended with a religious faith molded by a national culture.[2]

The full force of this statement is apparent when we realize that the German church under National Socialism was Miller's unspecified standard of comparison. In light of this captivity, H. Richard Niebuhr concluded that, "Only a new withdrawal followed by a new aggression can then save the church and restore to it the salt with which to savor society." Accordingly "the task of the present generation appears to lie in the liberation of the church from its bondage to a corrupt civilization."[3] Much of the balance of the essay is an eloquent description of that bondage and that corruption. Pauck concluded his essay with the hope that "a prophet will arise among us who ... will speak to us in the name of the living God with such power and authority that all who long for salvation will be compelled to listen."[4]

These essays were part of the attempt of neo-orthodox theologians in America to free the public party from the social gospel's dependence on liberal theology. Especially through the work of Reinhold Niebuhr, the prophet Pauck longed for, the doctrine of sin was brought to bear on social realities. No human institution, however democratic, deserved to be equated with the kingdom of God. Thus the public party attempted to extricate itself from its captivity to American civilization. In 1934 Reinhold Niebuhr wrote, "The war convinced me that religion can be effective only if it resists the embraces of civilization."[5]

But neo-orthodoxy did not affect the public party very profoundly. It was mostly a movement among intellectuals, and not among pastoral clergy. The public party eventually returned to its old line. Richard Niebuhr, one of the original opponents of culture-protestantism, offered a model for transforming culture which encouraged the same kind of hope for culture that had marked the old social gospel.[6]

Instead of recovering the original Protestant ideal of conforming culture to the kingdom of God, the public party reverted to working and hoping for "transformations." Reinhold Niebuhr's failure to reform the public party shows how little sympathy Americans have for tragedy as the last word on history. The idea of perfectability continues to haunt American social Christians.

Nor did neo-orthodoxy bring the public party any closer to a redefinition of the personal experience of conversion which had fallen by default to the control of the private party. Neo-orthodoxy was itself suspicious of "religious experience." That tended to leave the private lives of public-party adherents in the care of depth psychology since the public party would not work out its own theory of spiritual formation. Unable to embrace the piety of the private party and put off by that party's indifference to justice, neo-orthodoxy offered no alternative piety of its own. In time, each party returned to its accustomed style. After impressive initial salvos, neo-orthodoxy ended in an embarrassing hang fire. Neo-orthodoxy foundered on its incapacity to state a gospel for the self beyond typical American romantic illusion. American Protestantism left its people in a vulnerable state as World War II bore down on the churches. In the aftermath: "Among a people for whom it had been natural to blur the kingdom of God with society, the anxieties provoked by world politics would drive so much the deeper. Without reassurance short of tragedy, or a meaningful reconciliation beyond tragedy, helplessness and apathy might succeed among the doves, stupidity among the serpents, and among plain citizens still interested in private life, a final indifference to prophets, a new popularity of priests offering easy shelter."[7]

Postwar Evangelism and the Private Party

American Protestants were saved the agony of deciding whether to enter the war by Pearl Harbor. The opponents were so obviously the opposite of American democratic Christian civilization, that the commitment of the churches to the war was unhesitating. The churches suspended the servicing of their institutional needs for the duration. With the coming of peace, they took up evangelism for the sake of replenishing their memberships, but mass evangelism had been so discredited by the twenties that a new method was needed.

The churches developed visitation evangelism. They talked of a theology shaped to meet the fresh situation of the postwar, post-Protestant, pluralistic America; in practice they acted out the opposite. Protestants did not want to stand out. They wished to fit in. Visitation evangelism meant friends asked other friends to join church and confess Jesus Christ as Lord and Saviour. Each friend was free to attach what meaning he or she chose to the joining and to the confession. Common meanings consisted of an expression of gratitude for God's help in the war; hope for God's help in the tensions of postwar international politics; and a prayer for the blessing of God in getting back to the normal business of establishing families, pursuing careers, and improving living standards.

It was a surprisingly quiet and contentless celebration of religion, definitely not a Protestant revival. But perhaps that was to be expected in a society where Protestantism was no longer the "established religion." This movement was instead a revival of all kinds of religion, "a revival of *interest* in religion."[8] Any guru who hung out a sign got a response. President Eisenhower's famous offhand remark in 1954 was a suitable motto for the entire religious scene of the fifties. "Our government makes no sense unless it is founded on a deeply religious faith—*and I don't care what it is.*"[9]

Perhaps *the* common denominator among those faiths was that religion was offered for purposes which the devotee specified beforehand. Prominent among these prescribed purposes was peace of mind and confident living for an age of anxiety. Another common denominator was the absence of criticism of the American way of life, and support of it against atheistic communism. Dr. Billy Graham became the standard bearer of this decade of the private party. The message, little changed from the Third Awakening, carried even less molding force than before. It submitted to the needs of peace of soul, and more explicitly than ever to conservative politics.[10]

During Dr. Graham's 1955 New York City campaign, the Marble Collegiate Church of Norman Vincent Peale received the largest number of decision cards. This church was the chief center of Protestant positive thinking, and adherents of that brand of religion recognized it in Graham's message. One sermon, "Partners with God," which he repeated frequently, promised that by becoming a business partner with God, through stewardship and tithing, one could double or triple one's income.[11]

The evangelism of the fifties was easily the most bland in the history of awakenings in America. It made no attempt to adjust the message for the changed circumstances of the postwar world. It merely repeated the formula, somewhat less blatantly, which the private party had devised during its capitulation to the Gilded Age. So the revival of the fifties peopled the churches with members who used religion to avoid the necessity of responding to the major issues of their time. These issues included: the new role of America as a superpower among the nations; the demotion of Protestantism to merely one religious option for Americans among many; fates of native, black, and female Americans; the implications of advanced technology, symbolized in the bomb, for the well-being of the human family; and, finally, how to conceive of and experience the presence of God in so changed an American world.

The Sixties and Seventies

If the fifties belonged to the private party, the sixties were a revival for the public party. It then became even clearer that the public party was a minority among Protestants and that the concerns typical of the social-gospel tradition could have force in the churches and in society at large only when "protestants" outside in the general culture joined churchly Protestants in the protest. Civil rights for black Americans became the catalytic issue for the revival of public-party influence, and the rallying point for public-party types within the churches and their ideological colleagues in the liberal, Enlightenment wing of the culture outside.

Public-party whites in Protestant churches, with special direction and encouragement by the National Council of Churches, together with youths and liberals everywhere, joined the civil rights movement. The initial integrationist phase peaked in 1965, after which blacks took responsibility for their own leadership in partial repudiation of integrationist models. Puzzlement in the churches at the overtures of black power, together with the escalation of the Vietnam War, shunted attention of whites to the war. Thus ended the public-party decade.

The twofold heritage of the black power and the anti-war movements augured great changes for Protestantism as it entered the seventies. First, blacks' insistence that they be allowed their own culture further eroded the vision of a Christian civilization in America which Protestants assumed God had been endorsing since the beginning. And second, the rising generation, having witnessed the debacle of Vietnam, largely assumed that America could no longer claim to be God's chosen nation. Protestants are still trying to cope with the meaning of these repudiations of their traditional ideal of a Christian America.

The seventies saw a withdrawal from the activism of the sixties into a contemplative binge of "harmonial religion" from which Protestants have not yet recovered,[12] as the religious tenor of the country swung back to the inner piety of the fifties in contrast to the political piety of the sixties. The charismatic movement, for one, offered a resurgence of pentecostal religion to fill the experiential void left by a decade of political religion.

Perhaps the greatest contribution of the seventies will have been the suggestions for revising theology and life-style that came out of the women's liberation movement. This movement represented the most thoroughgoing "awakening," in the sense of a holistic adjustment to a new situation, of all the responses since World War II. The biblical and theological traditions of Protestantism were thoroughly overhauled as well as new consciousness and life-styles hammered out—but not necessarily as a seconding of the Protestant heritage. Indeed, the unqualified public-party endorsement of the women's rights movement, like its previous endorsement of revolutionary violence for blacks and Vietnam protestors, leaves the nagging suspicion that the controlling heritage is not classic Protestantism but classic Enlightenment liberalism.

The period from the collapse of the Third Great Awakening included through the seventies Protestant awakenings in only the most ironic sense. Each of the parties took turns applying their truncated forms of the Protestant adventure.

In the seventies the churches were left in confusion, withdrawal, and internal conflict. The churches had finessed their way past most major issues of the postwar world and the suspicion grew that the vitality had gone out of the Protestant adventure. It is up to Protestants to decide whether that suspicion is justified.

Given the maladjustment of the Third Awakening, and the nonadjustment of the sporadic revivals since then, Protestants have their work cut out for them. The most obvious place to start is with reforging the link between private piety and public compassion, broken in the Gilded Age. Only in the spirit of a newly whole Protestantism can there arise a witness faithful enough to deserve the attention of Americans inside and outside the churches.

Concluding Remarks: The Failure of American Protestant Eschatology

The story Protestants claimed to be writing from the beginning was nothing less than the final chapter of redemptive history. Jonathan Edwards gave that myth classic expression as the Great Awakening tapered off around him. Embarrassing as it may be to Edwards scholars, he delivered a series of sermons in 1739 that set out the context in which Edwards, its leader, understood the Awakening. Published after his death, it was called, *A History of the Work of Redemption.*[13] Today we expect only fundamentalist dispensationalists to match the events of the times to mysterious prophecies of the book of Revelation, but that was precisely what Edwards did.

On his reading of Revelation 16:16, the final chapter of redemptive history begins with the complete overthrow of Satan's hold on this world and the triumph of the church over all her enemies. That will introduce the kingdom of Christ on earth that will last one thousand years (Rev. 20:4). At the end of this millennium or thousand-year period there will be a brief apostasy followed by a general resurrection, the visible appearance of Christ to judge, and the displacing of this world by the world to come. There is no indication that Christ will be visibly or bodily present during the millennium. Instead He will reign through the victorious church. Edwards left little doubt that the way to begin this victory on earth was by revivals such as his congregation and New England had been experiencing, and that the next one might just be the swift beginning of a series of revivals that would gradually spread throughout the world. Edwards claimed not to know where this pouring out of Spirit for final victory might begin, but he allowed, "We know not . . . whether what has already taken place be not some forerunner and beginning of it."[14] In Northampton that meant that it was the task of his congregation to use all the means at its disposal to ignite revival again in hopes that it would turn out to be the beginning of the millennium. The opening sentence of the chapter from which the above quote was taken spoke of "how the success of Christ's redemption will be carried on." That coupled with his emphasis on "means" like "preaching . . . and the use of the ordinary means of grace" expose what has continued to be a fundamental motive of Protestants in America—they expect to *succeed* in establishing the kingdom of heaven in America by the force of their piety—with due recognition of the sovereignty of God.

Finney continued this tradition. We have already noted how at one point he expected the kingdom of God to come in the form of the millennium in three years. He expected it to come in the same way as Edwards had, through the medium of revivals. "If the whole church as a body had gone to work ten years ago . . . the millennium would have come in the United States before this day."[15] Here the characteristic note is again: American Protestants expect to *succeed* in bringing the kingdom of God in America by the force of their piety, and soon. The Protestant adventure in America was predicated on this expectation. When Protestants could no longer bank on such success, they lost heart and the adventure collapsed. The failure of the Protestant adventure has been the failure of its eschatology, of its understanding of how God's work comes to completion. They insist that it will happen soon in this world by means of their efforts, all the while claiming that biblical apocalyptic literature declares it so.

That is supremely ironic since the particular biblical literature Edwards and Finney cited had been designed precisely to explain the failure of attempts to set up the kingdom of God on earth. Apocalyptic means a form of literature that included a scheme for the final drama of history. Its Christian version usually included the following elements: the people of God would be persecuted almost to extinction; Christ would then appear out of heaven to stop the course of history; a general resurrection would occur; Christ would act as judge to separate all humankind to eternal punishment or eternal life; Christ would then take the righteous with Him into the world to come; this world would then pass away.

An apocalyptic version of the end of history took hold in Judaism when the cultural crusade of Alexander the Great threatened to snuff out the faithful in Jerusalem about 165 B.C. when the Book of Daniel was written. It flourished in New Testament times, especially in Mark's community, during the war of 66–70 A.D., and during the persecutions of the church of the Book of Revelation under the Roman emperor Domitian around 96 A.D. The supreme irony is that in their heady desire to find biblical warrant for their apparently imminent triumph, American Protestants turned to literature aimed at encouraging churches on the verge of imminent extinction, with the result that when the Protestant churches needed similar encouragement, they had exhausted through misuse the very literature they then most needed. It will be a central strategy of this book to turn again to one example of biblical apocalyptic literature and in using it for its intended purpose find the encouragement it can still give to a church shorn of expectations of triumph.

I suspect that if Protestants had been more candid, they would have admitted that their understanding of their role in history never did come from reading the biblical apocalyptic literature. They found their real story elsewhere in the Bible and then imposed it on the apocalyptic sections. The real sources of Protestant self-understanding lay in the history of Israel: the exodus (from Europe), the wilderness wanderings (survival years as colonists), the conquest of Canaan (destruction, displacement, and enslavement of native and black Americans), and the final emergence of Israel as a nation. That story (the revolution and after) fits the saga of Protestant dominion in America much better than the stories of the communities from which the apocalyptic literature was generated.

The history of Israel in the 200 years before the Roman destruction of the Temple fits the Protestant history in America even better, for it has become like late Judaism, an exile in its own land, fra .ented into parties, and finally more concerned for its survival than for its God-appointed mission. The hope is that one of those parties within late Judaism, the one that came to be called "Christian," can even now show us the way out of that exile back to our originating mission.

Part II

The Recovery of the Protestant Adventure

·6·

Dealing with the Demons

Images for Becoming Christian

The survey of the collapse of the American Protestant adventure has made our assignment clear: where in the New Testament can we find a form for the Christian experience that will overcome the limitations of the party forms? Of the two parties, only the private party has continued to pursue the reformation of persons. In so doing, it has taken over for its purposes two of the three major New Testament images for becoming Christian.

One of these is the image of "rebirth," from the Gospel of John—most particularly from the conversation with Nicodemus in which the Johannine Christ says, "You must be born anew" (Jn. 3:7). This image is so popular with private-party people that they call themselves "born-again Christians" to distinguish themselves from the rest of the church. This Johannine image is a fruitful one for understanding Christian existence. But because of its strong associations with private-party practice and doctrine, it is not a promising place to make a fresh start that aims at transcending party prejudice.

The same is true for the image taken from Paul, the Christian as a "new creation." "Therefore, if anyone is in Christ, he is a new creation; the old has passed away, behold, the new has come" (2 Cor. 5:17). The texts behind these images are so common in the history of private-party revivalism that many Protestants are able to hear them only with the accent and emphasis of a particular evangelist they have heard at some time in their lives. It is just these built-in associations with the private party that militate against their use as fresh starting points.

The third major image for Christian experience comes from the synoptic gospels, Matthew, Mark, and Luke. It is the image of discipleship. This image is relatively infrequently used by private-party types, in particular, or by Protestants in general. There have been two major exceptions. The most famous is the work by Dietrich Bonhoeffer, *The Cost of Discipleship*. In the original German, the title was simply *Discipleship*. The other exception is Karl Barth's use of the same image in explicit dependence on Bonhoeffer in his section of the *Church Dogmatics*, entitled "The Call to Discipleship."[1] Bonhoeffer's statement was very influential in neo-orthodox circles. But since neo-orthodox thought did not filter down into the life of the church, and since neo-orthodoxy shunned "religious experience" as such, the image of discipleship is relatively free of party associations. For this reason I am persuaded that the image of discipleship is a promising container for the new wine of Protestantism that aims to transcend private and public parties.

The Apocalyptic Connection

The image of discipleship occurs in all three of the synoptic gospels, but we shall concentrate our attention on Mark, not only because the idea of discipleship appears there first, but also because it appears there in a more apocalyptic context than in the others. We recall that apocalyptic literature concerns itself with the revelation of how history will end in the coming of the kingdom of God.[2] It first arose when a hostile culture was threatening to destroy Israel. As we have hinted, this nadir in Israel's history came when the cultural crusade for Alexander the Great turned Jerusalem into a

Hellenistic city with a charter that outlawed the law of Moses.[3] At this point around 165 A.D., a party arose in late Judaism called the *hasidim,* or separated ones, who preferred martyrdom to submission. Support for their response came through a new view of history that combined Israel's prophetic tradition with elements from Persian religion. This new view we call apocalyptic. It continued to affirm the prophets' promises of the final triumph of Israel, but transferred the scene of that victory to another world that would succeed this one. That entailed a new evaluation of this world. Although the hasidim continued to affirm the goodness of creation, they modified the traditional doctrine of God's control of history to allow for a temporary takeover by mythical opponents of God, namely, Satan and the demons. Their temporary dominion in the world accounted for the hostility of Hellenistic culture in Maccabean times, and for the tragic fate meted out to the faithful. The promise of resurrection to a life after death and a new world free of all evil enabled the *hasidim* to take their stand and continue their witness in the world.

The word apocalyptic has two unfortunate connotations which are not necesssary to the original idea. When we say apocalyptic, we usually mean "disaster" as in an apocalyptic end to the world that would accompany an all-out nuclear war. Biblical apocalyptic literature often includes a story of final disaster in history but the emphasis lies elsewhere. Humankind creates the final disaster, but God repairs that with new life in a new world. The emphasis is on what God does for the final redemption of the human race, not on what we have done to destroy ourselves and our world.

The second unfortunate connotation is to suppose that since the world and its culture have fallen into the hands of Satan, we must withdraw from the world into ascetic enclaves that devise holy cultures of their own in studied rejection of everything that characterizes the outside culture. To be sure, there were such communities in late Judaism as, for instance, the people of Qumran. But other heirs of apocalypticism in New Testament times, the Pharisees and the Zealots, found ways to engage the world actively and aggressively while they hammered out their own blend of Israelite heritage with Hellenistic culture—without sacrificing their identity to Hellenism in the process. Their foundation in apocalpytic thought made that possible. This same apocalytptic foundation made it possible for the Christian party within Judaism to hammer out its own distinctive blend. At its best, apocalyptic thought encourages engagement with the world, not sectarian withdrawal.

Late Judaism and Late Protestantism

The parallel between late Judaism and the situation of American Protestantism will, I hope, be obvious. In the Gilded Age, Protestants were challenged by an aggressive new scientific outlook that threatened to replace a God-centered universe with one that developed and operated according to laws intrinsic to a material universe in which the highest form of life was the human species. That same scientific world view offered a model for economic life that made the Protestant tradition of love of neighbor in the marketplace obsolete. A useful catchall title for this burgeoning culture would be scientific humanism. It had its historic roots in the Enlightenment tradition, a tradition which from the beginning of the American experience competed for domination with the Puritan tradition. Until the Gilded Age, American Protestants were sure that the Puritan strain would ultimately win in this competition. Then it began to dawn on Protestants that they might not win, that the promises of Protestant prophets for a Protestant kingdom of God in America might not come to pass. At that point the situation of Protestantism was similar to that of Judaism at the time of the Book of Daniel. The Hellenistic culture's challenge to Judaism was similar to scientific humanism's challenge to Protestantism. There were of course differences. Jews were threatened with martyrdom unless they paid homage. Protestants were threatened with being declared deviants in a world where before they had set the patterns for conformity, and with being excluded from the prosperity that the new scientific economics promised. Such a fate seemed nearly as bad to Protestants in the Gilded Age as martyrdom was for Jews in the Maccabean period.

The response of Protestantism was no more unified than that mustered by Judaism. Parties within late Judaism took tacks similar to the private and public parties. The Pharisees, like the private party, withdrew from active politics, emphasizing a personal code of conduct that set it off from the world. Zealots, like the public party, chose politics as their distinctive sphere and devised revolutionary strategies to regain power in the world. Both parties retained their hope of ultimate victory—Zealots by revolutionary political action, Pharisees by the power of their piety. These options seemed feasible until the Zealot program took the form of war against Rome in 66–70 A.D. That proved the Zealot program futile as Rome crushed the Jewish people and destroyed their city, temple, and national status. Pharisaism survived, but only by withdrawing from mission engagement with the world into a sectarian form of religion, chiefly concerned with its own survival.

At this point the Marcan community emerged with its own special version of apocalypticism. This led it to refuse participation in the Zealot war and to endure the persecution that threatened its survival, but also to refuse to withdraw even from so hostile a world. It found a way to be indifferent to survival while it enlarged its contact with and mission to Rome, the superpower of its day. It was able to manage this feat by its apocalyptic outlook and the path of discipleship that outlook engendered. Thus Mark was able to develop within the defeated, withdrawn people of God an option that was destined to have an overpowering influence in the same world culture from which Judaism felt forced to withdraw. In the hope that Protestantism might develop a similar option appropriate to our day we turn to Mark.

The Redaction-Critical Connection

In our consideration of the Gospel of Mark, we need to consciously distinguish our approach from that of the public party. A recent development within scholarly research has helped to overcome the shortcomings of the quest for the historical Jesus. At one time, in the attempt to recover the historical Jesus, it seemed necessary to assume that the primary value of the synoptic gospels was to provide access to the past ministry of Jesus. With the rise of redaction criticism,[4] it has now become clear that this assumption was quite out of keeping with the intention of the writers of those gospels. The synoptic editors or redactors, thus *redaction* criticism, arranged and shaped the pieces of tradition primarily so that the risen Christ would speak to their need in their time and only secondarily to reconstruct the ministry of the historical Jesus in his time. To read and interpret the gospels in the light of this primary intention of the editors or redactors is to practice redaction criticism. The good news was and is that the Jesus who seemed to be past was in truth alive and present for encounters with the reader. Indeed, the real point of the gospel stories is to offer the reader the same chance to meet and be inducted into discipleship by Jesus that the original companions of Jesus were offered. The familiar difficulty of fitting the gospels into genres of literature of the first century lies precisely here. In other historical literature the stories are really about the past, but in the synoptics, the stories are not to be read as a biography about Jesus. The stories are expected to reenact themselves in the times and places of the readers.

It was a pioneering, methodological breakthrough when Günther Bornkamm, the most prestigious current chronicler of the historical Jesus, saw in Matthew's story of the stilling of the storm "a kerygmatic paradigm of the danger and glory of discipleship," that is, a story about "the little ship of the Church,"[5] rather than a record of a past, a nature miracle isolated to a particular moment in time.

Clues to the Continuing Presence of Jesus

Mark, particularly, invited the reader to transpose the events about an apparently past Jesus into the situation of the witnessing community. This is the point of the admonition following the transfiguration. "And as they were coming down the mountain, he charged them to tell no one what they had seen until the Son of man should have risen from the dead" (Mark 9:9). The vision of the transformation of Jesus modeled the shift in perception that takes place once the reader of the book sees that the book is dealing with the resurrected Jesus. In other words, the risen, living, contemporary Son of man is none other than the Jesus of the gospel stories, only now transformed in the enlightened perception of the believing reader.

This meaning of the transfiguration is strengthened by the saying which immediately precedes it: "Truly, I say to you, there are some standing here who will not taste death before they see the kingdom of God come with power." Only Peter, James, and John "witness" the transfiguration. They are the "some." The recognition of the transformed Jesus as a heavenly being with powerful access to the reader's life is the meaning of "the kingdom of God come with power."

In fact the death and resurrection of Jesus turned out to be an advantage to the reader for they loosened Jesus from the past and allowed him to be powerfully present. This is the point of the speculation about the source of Jesus' power in Mark 6:14ff. Popular opinion (v.14b) and Herod himself were persuaded that the death and resurrection of John had released John's power into the ministry of Jesus. This parabolic speculation about the meaning of John's death misidentified John with Jesus, but it was correct in exposing the meaning of death and of resurrection as the path by which the power of past servants of God can continue in the present.

The speculation about transfer of power from one figure to another also explains the association of Jesus with Elijah (Mk. 6:15, 8:28). The idea of a second career for Elijah rests on the capacity of translation to bypass death and go directly to another life, making Elijah powerfully available at some later point in history. Just as Elijah through his translation became available at the transfiguration to succor Jesus in view of his impending martyrdom, so Jesus through his resurrection became available to succor his followers after he had supposedly, that is, historically, "gone." It was because of this belief in the continuing presence of past figures that the crowd believed that Elijah hovered over the crucifixion scene. In the misperception of the mocking onlookers that Jesus was calling on Elijah, and in their expectation that Elijah might "come to take him down," they witnessed to that common belief. The crowd was wrong about Elijah, but correct about the fashion in which past figures of redemptive history may continue to be present to God's people. Mark confirmed this idea of a continuing presence from the past, not by identifying Jesus with John or Elijah, but by identifying John with Elijah. "I tell you that Elijah has come..." (Mk. 9:13)

It was especially appropriate for the editor to put the question about a second appearance of Elijah just after Jesus' transfiguration since that episode had prefigured the same possibility of a second appearance for Jesus once he was risen ("He charged them to tell no one what they had seen, until the Son of man should have risen from the dead."). This explains the connection of the transfiguration story with the resurrection and with the explanation of John's ministry as Elijah of the past continuing in the present. So Mark used the story of the transfiguration as a parable of the way the historical Jesus of the past becomes the risen Christ of the present.

The final parable of the powerful presence of Jesus to the believing reader came in the form of the curious ending of Mark. The disciples were twice promised audiences with the resurrected Jesus in Galilee. ("I will go before you to Galilee," 14:28, and "he is going before you to Galilee; there you will see him, as he told you." 16:7) In the absence of standard resurrection appearances comforming to 1 Corinthians 15:3–5 or to the endings of Matthew and Luke, scholars wonder if perhaps Mark meant Jesus' second coming with these two promises. That is obviously not the intention, since the description of the final coming of the Son of man in chapter 13 makes it an appearance simultaneously present to the whole earth. A trip to Galilee would have been irrelevant to the Second Coming since it would not matter where on earth you were.

Then what does "going to Galilee" mean when no Galilean appearances are offered and when the editor seems finally to have cut off even that expectation by the failure of the women to relay the angel's message ("for trembling and astonishment had come upon them and they said nothing to any one...16:8.)? The most probable answer is that the Galilee where the risen Son of man may be seen and where he may go before one to lead in discipleship is the "Galilee" of the book of Mark. Mark began Jesus' ministry with the words "Jesus came into Galilee preaching the gospel of God..." In the words of the angel at the empty tomb, the reader is invited at the end of the book to go back to the beginning and read it again—only this time with the astonished awareness that the Jesus in the text is alive and offering the reader the same kind of experiences that seemed on first reading to have been past and gone. Some such perception of the author's intention is the logical outcome of the redaction-critical perspective and of the author's designation of his book as "good news" (1:1). We shall return to further explore this issue in the next chapter.

Private-Party Response to Redaction-Criticism

Unfortunately, the private party tends not to be open to the redaction-critical interpretation of the synoptics. Its doctrine of the literal inerrancy of Scripture commits it to an apology for the historical accuracy of the synoptic accounts, as though a meticulously accurate recounting of the events of Jesus' ministry just as they happened were the main intention of the authors or of the inspiring Spirit behind them. Ironically, this misperception of the character of the gospels tends to consign the Christ figure in them to a distant past just as effectively as the public party's quest for the historical Jesus tended to relegate him to the past. In one case the figure of Jesus is stripped of all relationship to faith, except perhaps as its presupposition. In the other case the Jesus figure is elaborately clothed in a full-blown Messianic self-consciousness, but placed beyond the reach of our present experience. No doubt this backlash of literalism is a major reason why the private party has relatively little use for discipleship as a model for its piety. If we accept my interpretation using the redaction-critical approach to the Jesus of Mark, what initial experience of Jesus does Mark offer for the contemporary reader?

"Come Out of the Man, You Unclean Spirit"

In the book of Mark the ministry of Jesus in Galilee begins with a summary statement that the kingdom of God was at hand (Mk. 1:14, 15). In the apocalyptic context of the book, that meant that the reign of forces in the world contrary to God was about to be displaced by an action of God. That posed the question for the reader, "What form will God's fresh intervention in the world assume?"

The first incident following the summary is the calling of the four fishermen (Mk. 1:16–20). Obviously the editor's placing of this incident immediately following the announcement of the theme of the kingdom gives it relevance to that theme. But the next episode best displays the apocalyptic flavor of the kingdom's coming. For Mark therefore it is better to begin with that episode and then return to the call of the four in light of it.

The next episode is an exorcism in the synagogue in Capernaum during a Sabbath synagogue service (Mk. 1:21–28). The allusions to teaching that come before and after the exorcism story (vv. 21–23 & v. 27) are the work of the editor who gave no hint of the content of the teaching. The point is to establish the character of Jesus' "authority." "With authority he commands even the unclean spirits, and they obey him" (Mk. 1:27b).

The key to the meaning of the exorcism episode is the seemingly innocuous word "rebuke" in verse 25. "But Jesus rebuked him (the unclean spirit), saying, 'Be silent and come out of him!' " A careful survey of the meaning of this word in

Qumran, Old Testament, and other Semitic literature, has shown conclusively that the underlying Hebrew word "is a technical term for the commanding word, uttered by God or his spokesman, by which evil powers are brought into submission, and the way is thereby prepared for the establishment of God's righteous rule in the world."[6]

Mark clearly intended to show in this powerful act of Jesus that it was precisely in the exorcisms that the kingdom of God had drawn near to a world otherwise under the domination of Satan. The demon expressed as much when he said, "Have you come to destroy us? I know who you are..." The demon recognized in Jesus' exorcising authority the beginning of the end of the domination of the world by forces opposing God's will. By this early manifestation of authority, Mark demonstrates the pattern Jesus' ministry will take. This explains why he included more exorcisms than either of the other two synoptic editors while they add none to his list. The editorial point is clear. Exorcism was the principle, public way the kingdom of God began to manifest its liberating power.

Resistance From Jerusalem to Jesus' Exorcisms

This editorial point with regard to exorcisms is confirmed and taken a step further by Jesus' response to the comment by scribes from Jerusalem that he cast out demons by the prince of demons (3:22–30). Following an editorial technique typical of the author, this discussion is bracketed within another episode—a similar but milder accusation by Jesus' family (3:19b–21) and Jesus' response to it (3:31–35).

In several ways the editor signals that this is an extremely important episode for him. He puts the misinterpretation of exorcisms in the mouths of Jesus' chief opponents, namely the scribes from Jerusalem. Although, the Pharisees and Herodians had already caucused to plan Jesus' end (3:6), they did so in Galilee where there was no power for capital punishment. Such power resided only in Jerusalem. Scribes from Jerusalem appear again in chapter 7 to gather material for the case against Jesus in connection with his setting aside of hand-washing and the distinction between kosher and nonkosher foods. When Jesus arrived in Jerusalem they were almost continually on hand: to plan his destruction in connection with the Temple cleansing (11:18); to challenge his authority (11:27); to plot his arrest and death (14:1); to send the crowd to seize him (14:43); to share in his condemnation (14:53); to consult on handing him over to Pilate (15:1); and finally to mock him on the cross (15:31). For Mark the scribes epitomize that human hardheartedness which is closed to the healing power of the kingdom that it is Jesus' messianic mission to usher into the world.

Exorcism, Mark's Favorite Paradigm

The editor's main point in responding to the accusations of the Jerusalem scribes was that the exorcisms are the most important examples of the coming of God's reign in the ministry of Jesus. By the same token exorcisms are Mark's favorite example of Jesus' messianic power. As we have noted, the apocalyptic context for understanding the Marcan form of good news gave Satan a heavy hand in the affairs of the world. From this point of view the kingdom of God began to have most obvious effect in the world when Jesus intervened in those places where the hand of Satan was most obvious.

The opening episodes of Mark's gospel all point to this understanding of exorcism as the most powerful expression of Jesus' saving power and messiahship. John the Baptist provided the first clue to the distinctive character of Jesus' messiahship by pointing to him as the one "who is mightier than I" (1:7). The next episode specified the nature of this "might": Jesus was baptized with the Holy Spirit. The apocalyptic dualistic context of the might of Jesus' messiahship accounts for the very next episode when the Spirit drives Jesus into the wilderness to be tempted by Satan. The forty days in the wilderness serve to test the might of the Spirit in Jesus to cope with the power of Satan in the world. The introduction to the gospel (1:1–13) culminates in this demonstration of Jesus' power to resist the power of the world represented by Satan.

This dualistic battle is carried through each of Jesus' parabolic defenses: kingdom against kingdom (v. 24); house against house (v. 25); Satan against Satan (v. 25); strong man against strong man (v. 27).[7] The language of "the strong man's house" in the last pair is a direct play on the testimony of John the Baptist to Jesus as the "stronger" one in 1:7. The Greek word is the same in each case. Satan is the strong one because he does rule in the world. Jesus is stronger because in the exorcisms he shows that God has begun to displace the rule of Satan.

This exposition of the centrality of the exorcism as the model form of the inbreaking kingdom of God explains the special emphasis in the closing saying about the unforgivable sin. Rejection of Jesus' exorcisms amounted to a rejection of the special way God chose to inaugurate the kingdom through Jesus. To reject the *way* God comes amounted to a rejection of God himself. It was this that made the sin "unforgivable" (v. 29). To cut oneself off from Jesus' exorcisms was to cut oneself off from God.

Connecting the idea of forgiveness with exorcisms reinforced the significance of exorcism as *the* model form of the kingdom drawing near. Forgiveness also provided a bridge between exorcism and the other healing miracles in Mark. In chapter two, Jesus' teaching was interrupted by a paralytic being let down through the roof. But instead of the expected healing, Jesus said to the paralytic, "My son, your sins are forgiven" (v. 5). Then in verse 9, Jesus equated his healings with forgiveness in the saying, "Which is easier, to say 'your sins are forgiven,' or to say, 'Rise, take up your cot and walk'?" Then Jesus healed the man.

The ideological intertwining of exorcisms with healing miracles is further confirmed by the healing of the deaf and dumb boy in chapter nine, whose illness is traced to a "dumb and deaf spirit." Even where the demonic cause is not specifically mentioned, we may assume that in Mark any illness was a sign of captivity to a world contrary to God's reign. Demon possession was merely the most dramatic form among others of the hold Satan had over human life in the world.

Nature Miracle as a Form of Exorcism

Another form of miracle in Mark is the nature miracle, which also has a connection with exorcism. The link is found in the story of the stilling of the storm at the end of chapter four (4:35–41). Jesus' calming of the wind and sea is described as a "rebuke," the same technical term we noted before designating exorcism as a process of preparing for God's reign. "And he awoke and *rebuked* the wind, and said to the sea, 'Peace! Be still!'" The word for "Be still" is also used in the first and model exorcism so that the technique as well as the designation for the action puts the calming of the storm in the same category as exorcisms. These links between storm and demon possession arise from a common setting in the theme of conflict between God and a resistant force in the world.

Long before the rise of apocalyptic dualism, ancient Israel borrowed the motif of the waters of chaos from Egyptian, Mesopotamian, and Canaanite literature. In order to create the world and to maintain his rule in it, the God of Israel had to subdue these waters. Against this background the sea and other "waters" connote resistance to God. Salvation and the confirmation of God's sovereignty in the world show themselves by overcoming these waters which, like Satan and the demons, obstruct the reign of God. Consequently eight of the thirteen occurrences of "rebuke" in the Old Testament in which "God is effecting eschatological judgment in order to bring to fulfillment his purpose on the earth" have to do with the rebuke of the waters of chaos.[8]

So when Jesus calmed the storm in chapter four, he exorcised the elemental forces opposed to God's kingdom which in ancient Old Testament imagery were the equivalent of the demons in New Testament times. When the editor had the crowd ask in awe, "Who then is this, that even the wind and sea obey him?" it implied the same identification of Jesus as the question of the demon in the first exorcism, "Have you come to destroy us?" The same exorcising association would of course have been in the editor's mind in the story of walking on the water and calming the wind in chapter six. In exorcisms, healings, and nature miracles, Mark showed Jesus to be the agent of the reassertion of God's reign in the world. We may fairly conclude that for Mark, demon possession, illness, guilt, and the powers in nature resistant to the plan of God were all traced to the reign of Satan in the world, and that at root they all required overpowering confrontation with Satan. Accordingly, Jesus qualified as the agent of God for meeting all of these kinds of resistance to the reign of God when he withstood Satan in the wilderness because Satan was behind them all. He did not need to be tested for each kind of miracle. Exorcism then is the most explicit and dramatic form of confrontation with Satan. All the other miracles were also exorcisms in less dramatic form in the sense that they delivered people from captivity to the world as an expression of the drawing near of God's reign.

Social Equivalents of "Possession"

What relevance has exorcism for American Protestants? In my opinion it has massive relevance as soon as we translate the symbols of Satan and the demons into equivalents of the American Protestant experience. In order to understand the meaning of the exorcisms for our time, we do not need to believe in a literal Satan and actual demons. If we recall the experience that led to appropriation of these symbols from Persian religion, we may allow a similar American experience to suggest substitute symbols from our environment while we maintain the meaning of the symbols we displace.

Satan and the demons stood for the forces in Palestinian culture opposed to the spirit of traditional Judaism. If we can locate forces in American culture that are opposed to the original vision of the Protestant adventure, we shall have met our equivalent of the demons. If we can point to behavior under compulsive domination by those forces, we shall have located our equivalent possession. Our equivalent exorcism would be deliverance from that compulsive behavior.

Sociologists help us to trace the process by which forces in culture come to threaten a culture's native religious heritages. Weber related the process to the problem of maintaining charismatic vitality once the originator of a religion had gone.[9] The founding charismatic leader establishes a religion by virtue of his supernatural, superhuman powers or qualities. The difficulty with charismatic qualities is that they are "outside the realm of everyday routine and the profane sphere." These qualities tend to be diluted and lost in subsequent generations in the process of housing religious movements in institutions and in relating the movement to everyday economic life. There seems to be a "law of gravity" about the charismatic element in all of societal life—that with time it falls prey to everyday, earthly life, and loses its original creative impulse. But before the charismatic element is completely grounded, it can transform aspects of the society in which it becomes routinized.

Weber is especially interesting for our purposes because he traced the interaction of Calvinistic Protestantism, the parent of American Protestantism, with the economic side of life. Eventually Protestantism succumbed to the cultural law of gravity. But before it did, Weber credited it with transforming economic life by its piety and with contributing to the rise of the capitalistic state. But its very success made it vulnerable. Economic relations do not permit exercise of specifically religious and charismatic motivation. Thus the more Calvinists carried forward their economic involvement, the less religious they became.[10] Indeed the Calvinist tended to produce an ethic of work that degenerated into a solemn duty to work incessantly long after the religious origins of that duty were forgotten.

The Effects of Contemporary Possession

The most perfect example Weber could find of this economic religion was, interestingly enough for our purposes, in the writing of that father figure of American culture, Benjamin Franklin. From Franklin, Weber took the original portrait of the American Protestant turned "workaholic"—the man whose hammering could be heard at five in the morning or at eight at night.[11] Weber's thesis was that Franklin's workaholic nature showed the transformed pattern of Puritan worldly asceticism *"only without the religious basis,* which by Franklin's time had died away" (italics mine). Weber described an intermediate stage on the way to this loss of religion by using the language of possession. Once the Protestant had contributed to the building of "the tremendous cosmos of the modern economic order," that order itself turned back on the Protestant to determine his life with "irresistible force." Insofar as Protestants continue to try to bring their religious heritage to bear on their economic responsibilities, "the idea of duty in one's calling prowls about in our lives like the ghost of dead religious beliefs."[12] When the spirit of religion has departed, all that is left to life is the pursuit of wealth, which, in Weber's opinion, finds "its highest development in the United States."

It is this capacity of cultures in general, and American Protestant culture in particular, to overwhelm, captivate, and possess its religious descendants that leads us to see in the American Protestant experience an equivalent of the first-century Jewish and Christian experience of a world vulnerable to the control of Satan and demons. It is a striking confirmation of our thesis that Weber should have called the modern economic order a "cosmos" and its power to determine the lives of all who are born into it "irresistible."[13] Weber's description of compulsive behavior in the economic sphere suggests a modern equivalent of demon possession.

Weber and other sociologists have noted a special tendency of modern industrial society to confine religion more and more to special institutions that have a smaller and smaller share of control over one's life, until ultimate meaning and its pursuit become almost entirely a private affair.[14] All of one's public behavior is controlled by the norms established and enforced in the various institutions to which specific functions are assigned by society. For example, economic and social life are carried on under sanctions and norms quite divorced from the spheres of personal religious meaning. In terms of demon possession, the effects of modern society parallel the situation of the Gadarene demoniac who was controlled not by one demon, but by a multitude of them (Mk. 5:1ff). Modern industrial society tends to have a separate performance control for each sector of life. As one moves from sphere to sphere in society, one comes under the successive control of many "demons." The effect is demonic in the sense that each area of performance exercises its own control over the person involved quite apart from the meaning of his or her life. Modern industrial society possesses us in the performance of most daily tasks.

The effect of modern society also resembles possession in the sense that most of us are not aware of the control. We continue to think of ourselves as concerned Protestants committed to the values of our religious tradition, whereas an examination in depth of our operational motives shows that we actually serve the culture's values of family, career, and standard of living.[15]

With time, this "demonic"—that is, unconscious, compulsive—behavior destroys the Protestant witness and dismantles the Protestant adventure. When our everyday actions no longer flow from what we say we believe as Protestants, those beliefs soon become merely "rhetorical"— that is, they are the verbal residue of a lost identity with little connection with our present lives.

Logically, we might conclude that we should drop out of Protestantism at that point at which our Protestant beliefs have become corpses—bodies from which the spirit has departed. Most of us do not take such a drastic step because there is a shadowy security and identity even in rhetoric. And there are other advantages in belonging to a respectable and prestigious congregation of our peers after our specifically religious interests have faded. Despite these advantages, more and more Protestant church members are simply dropping out. Rhetoric is wearing thin.

However long Protestant parents may hang on to Protestant institutions, their children do not show the same loyalty. They take note of the merely rhetorical value of their parents' faith in contrast to their actual life-style. Perhaps the adult generation with rhetorical faith will stick with its rhetoric until the end, but their children are not likely to do so. They find that it takes little effort to jettison what to them has come to be just excess baggage and parental hangups.

The Need to be Exorcised

We see through the eyes of sociologists that contemporary Protestantism suffers under compulsive behavior that is a striking equivalent to first-century demon possession. This possession reflects a modern world fully equivalent in captivating power to the first-century world permeated by Satan and his demons. I do not explain our world with the mythology of Satan and the demons. This change in myth and symbol springs from an important break with one aspect of the first-century world view. The first-century myth allowed its inhabitants to shift the responsibility for their plight onto others—Satan and the demons. We now see that we must ourselves take the blame we used to lay on Satan. Perhaps the key insight preparatory to the exorcism of American Protestants is to own up to the fact that the "world" that possesses us is largely of our own making. Satan and the demons are ancient symbols for the compulsive power that "social constructions of reality" have over their inhabitants. Awareness does not of itself automatically release us from that power; it does point the way, however, to a modern equivalent of healing by exorcism.

Among Protestants, the private party will tend to resist this symbolic shift. It seems to contradict the literal inerrancy of the New Testament. I submit that the vast majority of private-party members have already made the move I am suggesting when they visit their family physicians instead of faith healers. They share with their physicians the assumption that microbes cause most illness and not demons. That assumption is just as contradictory of the New Testament as the one I am suggesting. When a private-party Protestant is willing to acknowledge microbes but does not take the correlative step of recognizing that human systems underlie an evil social world, he or she reveals a party prejudice about the world.

This prejudice was a cornerstone in the foundation of the private party. In the Gilded Age the private party used the New Testament view of a satanic world to escape responsibility for the emerging American world of advanced industrial society coupled with the laissez-faire economics that it was helping to construct. Its position was that the world was too evil to change, but too good to miss. The mythology of Satan and the demons seems to justify that position. I do not think it does. Instead it serves as another weary example in a long tradition of clinging to the letter of the New Testament in order to escape the spirit of its teaching. In my opinion it amounts to a modern equivalent of *corban*. If a Jew in Jesus' day declared that the money he would otherwise have given to support his parents was dedicated to the Temple, he escaped responsibility for his parents. Today private-party types declare their religious devotion to a biblical literalism that allows them to escape responsibility for collaborating in constructing and maintaining a social and economic system indifferent to the well-being of vast numbers of neighbors for whom we are responsible in love. Jesus' comment applies in both cases: "You leave the commandments of God and hold fast the traditions of men" (Mk. 7:8).

If we are willing, we now see that this God-contrary world has been of our own creation and not that of a fallen host of angelic beings. This world of our making then takes on a collective life of its own that turns upon us with a possessing power. Accordingly, Satan and his demons now appear as symbols of the power embedded in our social constructions of reality; their power is really the power of social systems. While a social system remains in force, release from it requires exorcism: that is where one must begin. But ultimately, social systems under the sign of Satan and the demons require social *re*construction—and as long as the symbols continue to be taken literally, we conveniently escape the responsibility for that reconstruction. This analysis shows how private party's insistence on literal belief in

Satan tends to serve that party's avoidance of responsibility for social change and its preservation of the status quo under the guise of fidelity to religious tradition. Having made the point that the fundamental reference of the mythology of Satan and the demons is social, we may risk dealing with the individual experience of exorcism in the hope that its social counterpart will not be submerged in the process.

Jesus, the Stronger One

When we begin to realize that the power of Satan and the demons is the power of culture, and that culture is a human creation, the temptation is to suppose that since we caused the problem, we can solve it.

At this point the public party is prey to its special prejudices. It has embraced the modern insight about the human construction of social reality. However, it assumes that wherever society may have deformed human life, society also has the power to transform it. It also tends to assume that this transformation of social reality will automatically bring with it the exorcism of the inhabitants of that society.

Nothing could be further from the truth of the gospel. When we awaken to the problem, we are already captive to it. Someone has described the situation of children as slaves and beggars to their environment. This is true. Children are defenseless in face of societal programming. But by the time we reach the age of discretion and responsibility, the values and life-style of the world have already impressed themselves on us so powerfully that we have no choice but to live out of them. Even in moments of rebellion we are counterdependent; when we wish to reject our programming, we are impotent to imagine workable alternatives or unable to construct and implement them. The typical radical can only imagine utopia—that is, no place. So with time, most radicals return to the familiar world, because it is the only world within human range. This has proved to be the story of most radicalism in the sixties and seventies. The terrorists of the seventies have kept alive their hatred of the status quo, but they have lost all capacity to generate real alternatives. This is counterdependence in its most tragic form. Hatred plus impotence breeds pure destruction. And still there is no freedom—only violent gestures of protest. What the terrorist displays in dramatic form is a parable of the frustrating captivity of us all.

Where may we turn in a world we have made but which we are powerless to remake or escape? Within the world, our captivity and impotence comes from our attachment to the formative, parenting figures in our personal biographies who have been the media through whom the world has programmed us. They lend to social constructions their emotional force. In our attachment to these formative figures, values and life-styles of the world take on inner, psychic power. So long as values and life-styles remain disembodied abstractions, they have no power over us. It is when they become incarnate in important persons close to us that they become unavoidably persuasive and compelling. Our important persons model the world for us; it is through them that the world fastens itself upon us. In the context of our deep attachment to them, the values and life-styles of the world present themselves as good news. In them we are seduced to the ways of the world. The power of the world over us is the power of the personal relationships we have had with the formative persons of our biographies. Through these formative persons we become possessed.

The way out of this possession must follow a process similar to the way in. We must find a person not captive to the world's values and life-styles. We must discover a person who is the medium for a lively, alternative world. We must discover a person who can displace the influence of the formative people in our biographies without repossessing us again to a parental world. We must come close to and know this new formative person so that an alternative to the world can possess us and become for us the new good news. That person is the Christ of the synoptics who offers himself in parable form as the figure of Jesus.

Jesus offers himself the way the editor of Mark offers him. To begin with, he is the one who is stronger than all the powerful influences that have ever come to bear on us through the formative figures of our biographies. Because he is stronger, he can pry us free of their compelling influence and of the captivating influence the world has had through them. This is the meaning of the exorcisms as the first of the powerful acts of Jesus' ministry in Mark. Through Mark, Jesus announces that there is an alternative to the ways of the world: the kingdom of God. But that remains a mild abstraction until embodied in a person through whom that alternative takes on incarnate power. The first moves of such a person must somehow demonstrate that he really is stronger than all the formative persons we have known before him. That is what Jesus demonstrates in the exorcisms.

The exorcisms promise the reader that Jesus is able to displace all the unfortunate dominating influences of his or her biography, thus opening up to the reader for the first time the possibility of a fresh beginning. This capacity of Jesus to free us from the captivating influence of the world through the formative figures of our biographies was what John the Baptist meant when he promised in Jesus someone stronger (Mk. 1:7). John went on to say that this strength would be shared in the Holy Spirit.

The Holy Spirit symbolizes the dimension of power in the kingdom of God. As we suggested, the world's values and life-styles cease to be abstractions and become powerful influences only when they are compellingly embodied in a person. The same is true of the kingdom of God, the alternative to the world. Only when the kingdom of God became embodied in Jesus did it become powerfully available to attract and influence us. The descent of the Spirit on Jesus at the time of his baptism represented the kingdom of God coming to life powerfully through the medium of the person of Jesus. In the exorcism, the possessing demons identified Jesus exactly in terms of this powerful channeling of the

Kingdom: "Have you come to destroy us?" (Mk. 1:24). For Jesus to be the powerful channel of the kingdom meant the destruction in the world of the influence of Satan and the demons. Once Mark has clearly identified Jesus as the match for all the cosmic forces that enslave humans to God-contrary purposes, it makes sense when the reader comes to the fifth chapter for the Gerasene demoniac to *run* to Jesus as soon as he sees him, out of reverence for him as the one strong enough to free him of his possession (Mk. 5:6).

Naming the Demons

Jesus' healings display a certain amount of technique. The early church probably used the miracle stories as a guide for those who were especially commissioned to continue the ministry of miracles in Jesus' name. Mark's own community no doubt continued the ministry of exorcism. The story of the strange exorcist casting out demons in Jesus' name (9:38–41) is most probably an autobiographical note from Mark's community.

Only Mark has the note on technique attached to the story of the epileptic boy whom the disciples could not cure while Jesus was on the mount of transfiguration with Peter, James, and John. In response to the question, "Why could we not cast it out?" only Mark has, "This kind cannot be driven out by anything but prayer" (9:29).

One item of technique is especially important for our adaptation of the symbolism of exorcism. That item is the naming of the demon. It occurs in the story of the Gerasene demoniac. This feature points to the fact that while captivity to the world of Satan and the demons is a common experience for us all, that captivity takes particular shape in each of our biographies. Typically our initial relationship with Christ as the Stronger One forms around the pivotal point of our particular "demon." Recalling that exorcism distinguished itself from other healings by the presence of a pattern of "seizure," one's demon is the place in one's life where the destructive effects of programming by the world take the greatest toll. This specific possession usually includes an inability to alter the behavior that continually leads to those effects.

Each "possessed" person will know best what his or her demon is, but the history of the Protestant adventure in America and the typical effects of modern culture on religion do suggest some themes.

The Work Demon

Martin Marty has pointed out for us how in the Gilded Age, Protestants concentrated their attention on a manipulation of economic values that led to the until then unheard-of equation of the glory of God with getting rich. From this point on, the main aim of Protestant life became the continuous increase of income. That meant a renewed and grotesque emphasis on the economic virtue of diligence. The longer and harder one worked, the more surely his, and now also her, income would rise. Increased income would bring the status and sense of self-worth that the world bestows on its achievers. The possessed Protestant we are describing is the workaholic. The "seizure" aspect of this demon comes in connection with the neglect of other values to which the workaholic declares he or she is deeply committed. This person typically says that so much work effort is for the sake of the spouse and family. But the spouse and family experience the work of the workaholic as depriving them of their need for the time, attention, and affection of the breadwinner. In many cases the spouse and family come to dread the workaholic's next promotion. When promotion comes, it is almost standard etiquette for friends to congratulate the rising achiever and at the same time to offer condolences to the newly deprived family. Workaholics in effect simulate one-parent families, with the accompanying trauma to the children. But the trauma is exacerbated by the fact that the neglectful parent is in residence; for even when physically present, the workaholic is merely between appointments, or absorbed in the bulging briefcase. With both parents working, it is possible for a pair of workaholics effectively to divorce one another and orphan their children while sustaining the forms of marriage and family.

Another "seizure" aspect of the "demon" of work is that the income for which the workaholic slaves is never enough, no matter how large it may become. Even when the spouse and family plead that they have all they need and more, it does not deter the diligent Protestant who continues to "spread the sound of his or her hammer at five in the morning until eight at night."

The third demonic dimension typical of compulsive Protestantism relates to the process and products of work itself. Compulsively diligent Protestants tend toward the same indifference to human well-being at work as at home. The effect of one's behavior on coworkers, of the production process on the workers and on the physical and human environment around the plant, and the effects of the product or service on the consumer are all subordinated to a "demonic" devotion to the company's upward mobility. Moreover the tendency of the modern industrial process to poison persons associated with it and to destroy the environment is as well documented as modern society's tendency to destroy the family. For so many Protestants to be so deeply engaged in the design and management of that process without seeming to care about, let alone protest, its inhumane effects, can best be understood in terms of the symbol "demon possession."

The final tragedy of demonic captivity to work comes when the captive is suddenly "set free" because of age or ill health. Without the fix of continuous and demanding work, the demoniac's life collapses and he or she suffers psychic death. The event of actual physical death, however long it may take in coming, is an anticlimax.

The good news is that the Christ who is stronger than the chaos of ancient Mesopotamian culture and the demons of Hellenistic culture is also stronger than the chaos and demons of modern industrial society. New life begins for possessed Protestants with enough residual sanity to recognize this stronger Jesus when, like the Gerasene demoniac, they run to him with reverent expectation.

The Consumption Demon

The demon of compulsive work represents the triumph of the economic virtue of diligence over the religious virtue of caring. The companion demon to compulsive work in modern culture is the demon of consumption. With the increasing productivity of advanced, industrial technology, the ability to produce goods and services threatens to outstrip our capacity to consume them. Unless some of us became willing to match the workaholics' productivity with an equal devotion to consumption, the whole world was threatened. So modern industrial society, via the media and advertising, made a massive offer which most Protestants could not refuse. The traditional Protestant mania to earn is now matched by a Protestant mania to spend.

As a young man, wondering about an adequate starting salary, I asked my pastor "How much does it cost to live?" I expected some kind of figure in reply. His answer instead was, "All you make!" One of the chief symptoms of the demon of consumption is the recurring surprise at the end of each pay period that you have spent more than you earned— *again!* The Gospel of Wealth in the critical period of 1875–1900 was matched at some point in the twenties with a companion Gospel of Consumption. The message of that gospel is that the solution to life's problems is to consume something. The world of Satan and the demons cues its goods and services to the natural appetites of eating, drinking, sexuality, acquisitiveness, and territoriality, as well as to psychological moods such as loneliness, anxiety, boredom, and depression. By coupling consumption with these recurring psychic states or felt needs, and where possible pampering them into grotesque proportions, the world sells its goods and services while minimizing conscious, volitional participation of the consumer. The idea is to get people to consume on impulse for unconscious reasons. The result is a modern equivalent of possession.

Presently in our society one of the chief symptoms of such possession, besides the overdraft, is obesity. Our sense of stress, depression, and boredom are cued to a vast industrial pantry of prepared "foods" that can be consumed with so little thought and effort that the demoniac is hardly aware that he or she has actually swallowed something. The resulting obesity has spawned a multibillion-dollar industry selling diets to the obese. At this point the "possession" becomes most obvious because only 5 percent of those who lose weight hold their slimmer selves; 95 percent are recycled into the overeating syndrome. The dieting itself turns out to be one more consumable. But obesity is only the most obvious example of possession. A society that regularly overspends its income and is in hock to the future shows that its whole pattern of buying is a form of possession.

Just as the demon of compulsive work affects the family, so the demon of consumption draws the family into its orbit. Indeed the demon of consumption hovers over typical Protestant family life. It was not by chance that Dean Hoge's survey found the preoccupying big three for Protestants to be family, career, and standard of living. They are an interlocking triangle. The supporting argument for the triangle claims that the breadwinner pursues his or her career for the sake of a rising standard of living for the family. In turn the family supplies the launching pad and support system for the breadwinner. This leads to the neglect of the emotional, caring needs of family life. As a surrogate to real emotional fulfillment, the family takes on the responsibility of pursuing the rising standard of living. Indeed it is the assigned responsibility of the family to see that its consumption keeps pace with the increased income. The overwhelming function that the family assumes is that of a school for obsessive consumption.

In preaffluent America the Protestant family devoted itself mainly to production. Now it is mainly devoted to consumption. Children are thus typically raised as gourmet and connoisseur consumers, while often they learn relatively little at home about work. The parents vaguely perceive that this uneven distribution of roles for production and consumption threatens to disable the rising generation for the work it must perform in order to support the life-style to which it has become accustomed.

Perhaps the most demonic aspect of the process of stimulating consumption turns on the continual transformation of frivolous wants into imperious needs and the accompanying promise of satisfaction—which of course must never be fulfilled. Otherwise the expanding inventory of new products to meet new "needs" would lie in warehouses unconsumed, and modern industrial, technological society would grind to a halt. As we saw in the case of the old-world view that saw evil as the work of Satan and the demons, possession was part of a cosmic system. The possession of consumption fits into the "cosmos" of modern culture: exorcism that would lead to reduced consumption will cause as much turmoil as it did in its ancient counterpart, where demons thrashed and screamed at the approach of the exorcist. "And crying out with a loud voice, he [the demon] said, 'What have you to do with me, Jesus, Son of the Most High God? I adjure you by God, do not torment me'" (Mk. 5:7). In fact, even then the economic implications of exorcism symbolized in the drowned swine led the people of Gadara to plead with Jesus to leave.

It will be relatively easy for public-party Protestants to identify the demons of compulsive diligence and compulsive consumption, since in principle this party is critical of the modern cosmos and sensitive to its "demonic" aspects. That does not mean these demons will thereby be any more manageable for public-party types. As Hoge pointed out, the big three of family, career, and standard of living captivate Protestants of whatever party stripe. All Protestants tend to lose their souls on their way to work and on their way to Sears—or wherever America shops. But awareness is an important step in the process of exorcism. And here the public party has an advantage.

The Sexual Demon

With respect to one demon that haunts modern American culture, the connections of the public party put their devotees at a disadvantage. I mean the demon of autonomous sexuality. Luckman makes the acute observation that although the different institutional segments of modern society, such as education, politics, and economics, exercise control over performance in their respective spheres, they do not thereby automatically capture consciousness in the personal realms that modern institutions ignore.[16] While accepting controls for the sake of the rewards that political and economic institutions have to offer, the citizen or worker may keep him- or herself personally aloof in that cool, laid back, elaborately uninvolved style that is so much a part of being urbane. Sensing that institutions are out to exploit, the sophisticate turns the tables on the world by withholding the true self and using the institutions as bases for personal projects. This is done in the hope that in the hard-won personal privacy where one retains control, personal meaning may be found and enjoyed.

One obvious private sphere where it is possible to explore and enjoy personal meaning is sexuality. Here is an area where one may be deeply and personally involved without the sense of capitulating to the alienating controls of social institutions. Control is a crucial issue here, for the institutionally alienated devotee of personal meaning has learned one thing in the world, if nothing else: that life and meaning belong only to the autonomous, to those who maintain control of their own lives in the personal sphere. The price of freedom is eternal vigilance against loss of this control to others.

The most obvious threat to autonomy in sexuality comes from the sexual partner. If he or she is allowed to intrude on personal autonomy the game is lost and one falls prey to the control of others—just the fate the urbane sophisticate hopes so fervently to avoid in all areas of life. So sexuality must be painstakingly disengaged from covenantal commitments except those of the most limited duration, and even then with built-in escape clauses. Sexual relationships are only worth continuing so long as they continue to contribute to private satisfaction, growth, and self-fulfillment. When partners falter in this service or when another partner offers greater prospect for fulfillment, one must be free to move on. Marriage contracts are no exception.

Next to binding covenants, the greatest threat to private meaning in autonomous sexuality is the regulations that culture, and most especially traditional religion, regularly attempts to bring to sexuality. In the great Christian tradition of sexuality, one loses one's autonomy to the partner in a lifelong commitment for better or for worse, and the new indissoluble union loses its autonomy to the Lord of life who regulates marriage for the ends of the kingdom of God. Only in this context does sexuality become a channel for true satisfaction, fulfillment, and meaning. Such regulation by traditional Christianity is anathema to the Protestant possessed by the demon of autonomous sexuality. The two roots of the word "autonomous" are "self" and "law," so that one heavy connotation of the word is that to be autonomous, one must be a law unto oneself. One of the marks of possession by this demon is the intricate exegetical and theological gymnastics through which public-party Protestants often put themselves in order to parlay freedom from the law in the name of the gospel into an autonomous sexuality that is completely contrary to the spirit of the gospel.

A standard interpretational ploy is to declare that the teaching of Jesus on sexuality was a time-bound function of an outmoded extended-family kinship system designed to preserve a social institution that is now obviously obsolete. Hence gospel regulation of sexuality passed with the extended Jewish family. It is hard to imagine a more ludicrous interpretation, since Jesus rejected his own family and redefined family in terms of doing the will of God. He could hardly have formulated the will of God for sexuality for the sake of the traditional Jewish family, which he himself relativized.

The "seizure" aspect of autonomous sexuality is most

evident, however, in the bogus experience of transcendence it offers. The danger of the cool, laid back style of the autonomous search for meaning is that one finds oneself finally alone. The advantage of sexuality is that it does involve an "other." The ultimate demonic possibility lurks in the *substitution* of the experience of transcending self in sexual liaison for a self-transcending experience with God. I suspect that many public-party Protestants have filled the void left by the rejection of private-party piety with the piety of transcendant sexual union. It is not an adequate substitute. Sexuality cannot bear the weight. The continual attribution to it of such weight in practice only promotes obsessive, demonic sexuality.

Exorcism, Vestibule to Discipleship

This sampling of current demons suggests the kind of identification that is necessary to inaugurate exorcism. Having named the demon, the next step is to put oneself into the hands of Jesus, the one who is stronger than possession.

At this point it is necessary to allow Jesus to take control of one's life and fate. It is in this relinquishing of control that our version of exorcism becomes the vestibule of discipleship. Jesus, the exorcist, then leads us on to Jesus the teacher— Lord of discipleship. The man cured of the legion of demons symbolized the progression. After having been cured and restored to his right mind, "The man who had been possessed with demons begged him [Jesus] that he might be with him" (Mk. 5:18). Rightly perceived, exorcism leads to discipleship. But before we make that transition, we need to look at a misperception of exorcism that blocks the way to discipleship.

Exorcism and Magic

When in Mark the scribes from Jerusalem spread the rumor that Jesus cast out demons by the prince of demons, that was tantamount to saying that Jesus' miracles were a form of magic. For our purposes I will define magic as the attempt to manipulate powers in the transcendent world to do one's bidding in this world. The key is to know the secret catchword or technique by which one can tap superhuman resources for one's own purposes. This is a well-known form of primitive, popular religion that always waits in the wings to displace higher forms of religion when they lose their credibility.

Bryan Wilson calls the religion of magic "thaumaturgy." His definition helps pinpoint the misuse of the exorcism tradition we are attempting to isolate. Thaumaturgical religion involves a narrow and essentially particularistic concept of salvation.

> The individual's concern is relief from present and specific ills by special dispensations. The demand for supernatural help is personal and local: its operation is magical. Salvation is immediate but has no general application beyond the given case and others like it.... Healing, assuagement of grief, restoration after loss, and the guarantee of external (or at least continuing) life after death are elements of the salvation which is sought.... Miracles and oracles, *rather than the comprehension of new principles about life*, are the instruments of salvation in this case.[17]

Wilson suggests out of an examination of contemporary third-world religions that whenever religions that expect an imminent transforming intervention into history by the gods are disappointed, they fall back on thaumaturgical religion as an alternative. The earliest church expected such a transforming intervention in the form of the return of Christ. Did its delay produce a magical backlash in the synoptic tradition? Form critics have indeed found parallels between the miracle stories of the synoptic tradition and the miracles of Hellenistic thaumaturgical religion. With this similarity in mind some New Testament scholars even suppose that the miracles of the gospel tradition are to be understood in the context of thaumaturgical religion, and that they were relayed to impress readers with the magical power of Jesus.[18]

This is precisely what the miracles, including the exorcisms, were not intended to convey. Wherever people sought from Jesus a miracle for a miracle's sake, he could not (Mk. 6:1–6) or would not (Mk. 8:11–13) oblige. Jesus only performed miracles in the context of the coming reign of God. Except as illustrations of this coming reign, the miracles are misleading. The essence of the coming kingdom is that God takes charge of life in opposition to the powers of the world. This is the opposite of magic, which seeks to take charge of God for conformity to the world.

The private party within Protestantism is always threatened with this distortion of Jesus' miracles. Because their party policy rejects the world-reforming thrust of the gospel, their merely personal religion is left to the mercy of the world and especially of the social and economic policies whose underlying motive force is blind to the demands of justice. Personal religion tends to become, among other things, a device for worldly success. We recall Billy Graham's gargoyle sermon "Partners with God," in which stewardship and tithing contribute to doubling or tripling one's income. Oral Roberts has a similar plan for "stewardship." This encourages thaumaturgical religion, that is, the manipulation of God for one's own success. In such tendencies to distort the gospel tradition, Graham, Peale, and Roberts are following a popular trend in current American religion; Ahlstrom has dubbed it "harmonial religion." He says, "Harmonial religion encompasses those forms of piety and belief in which spiritual composure, physical health, and even economic well-being are understood to flow from a person's rapport with the cosmos."[19] This is gentle language for a modern-day equivalent of Hellenistic thaumaturgical religion or—to put it more bluntly—magic.

A true contemporary equivalent of exorcism does not seek merely harmony with the cosmos. Exorcism leads the possessed to see the world for what it is, to break with it, and eventually, in discipleship, to seek to change it. Each modern "demon" is but one facet of a cultural "cosmos" that opposes the life of the kingdom of God. Neither the projects nor the rewards of the world as it stands, fit in with exorcism by

Jesus. Whoever hopes to use the power of Jesus to enhance career, standard of living, or mental poise devoted to worldly goals engages in magic and takes leave of the God of the kingdom of Jesus' teaching. There are many such religious options available in America now. Private-party piety has been bedeviled with this tendency ever since the Gilded Age, when it tried to mix the Protestant adventure with the gospel of wealth. The gospel of Jesus declares that they do not mix— one cannot serve God and mammon. Those who attempt to use the power of Jesus to do so are not undergoing exorcism, they are instead deepening their possession.

In the process of exorcism once Jesus names the demon, he casts it out. Exorcism is not an invitation to a thrashing expenditure of one's own energy to overcome the demon by new purpose and moral effort. In psychic fact the powerful grip of the demon is a power it has borrowed from all the formative persons through whom the world has fastened the demon on one's back. The programming of those persons in one's life cannot be exorcised by an act of will. They can only be neutralized by being displaced by someone more important. To put oneself and one's destiny into the hand of Jesus as *the* formative figure in one's life, to surrender in trust to his gentle control—that releases the grip of the demon. Freedom from the demons is not experienced as a reward for struggle. It is experienced as a gift from One who is stronger than the demons.

This translates to mean that Jesus is stronger than the God-contrary programming of our past. To be freed from that past is the same as forgiveness. Which is easier to say: "We are freed from our demon" or "We are forgiven"? It does not matter. They are both true at the same time.

But if exorcism means relinquishing of control in our lives to Jesus, what will he do with us? Where will he lead us? These questions prompt the major experience with Jesus that Mark offers us. We noted in connection with radical alien-ation that escape from captivity to the world "hangs fire" unless there is an alternative world, some place to fill the void of the "no place" of radical utopias. That place is discipleship.

·7·

Discipleship

Mark's Apocalyptic Context

Discipleship is the synoptic gospels' way of describing what it means to be a Christian. It is the companion image in the New Testament to John's "being born again" (Jn. 3:7) and to Paul's "new creature" in Christ (2 Cor. 5:17). As I said before, discipleship has the advantage for us of being relatively free from party prejudice, as a result, I think it has the possibility of becoming the vehicle for a recovery of a fresh Protestant identity.

Mark introduced the Call of the Four (1:16–20) as his first illustration of the verses that immediately precede it (1:14, 15) which set the theme of the coming kingdom. By this editorial arrangement the author was saying that what happened to these fishermen in being called is a primary way "the kingdom of God has drawn near." Since "kingdom of God" is synoptic language for redemption or salvation, to experience the nearness of the kingdom of God in the form of discipleship is the equivalent of "being saved" in private-party jargon.

Ever since the publication in 1892 of Johannes Weiss's book on Jesus' preaching of the kingdom of God, there has been a growing consensus among scholars that for Jesus the kingdom of God was an apocalyptic idea.[1] In this connection *apocalyptic* means that the kingdom of God is the dualistic counterpart to the world. A similar consensus is growing that would understand the gospel of Mark in the same way.[2] Indeed Mark puts the climax of Jesus' teaching to his disciples in the "little Apocalypse" of chapter 13, where his final christology is seen in the apocalyptic Son of man. It is impossible to escape the overall apocalyptic flavor of Mark's theology.[3]

The problem for American Protestants is that party prejudices die hard even when biblical scholars have solid information that contradicts them. Public-party Protestants still see the kingdom at home in the world and sketch plans for the new City of God, expecting it to emerge in the world whenever the participatory (or revolutionary) mix is just right.[4] Private-party evangelists claim to agree with apocalyptic dualism's estimate of the world by declaring that the Lord is coming soon. Meanwhile some of their chief representatives are reluctant to share with the public just how many millions they have invested in a world supposedly passing away!

For Mark, the world is indeed passing. The coming of the kingdom will climax with the return of the Son of man on clouds of glory (13:24–27; 8:38, 9:1). Mark's community expected that to happen any day (13:28–36). And when the Son of man comes, this world will simply be declared obsolete as the Son of man gathered his elect and moved with them into the "age to come" (10:30).

But the exorcisms and the schema of the End make dramatically clear that any drawing near of the kingdom must be an interruption of the world's usual business. The statement about the kingdom just preceding the Call of the Four makes that clear. *Kairos*, the Greek word that Mark uses for "time" in the phrase "the time is fulfilled," means the propitious moment in God's design which separates that moment from the flow of ordinary, chronological time. When *that* kind of time "is fulfilled and the kingdom of God has drawn near," every instance of the kingdom's coming must intrude upon the ordinary everyday projects of life that are coupled to the flow of clockwork time. The exorcisms and the

108 / Recovery of the Protestant Adventure

allied miracles of healing and storm-stilling were just such intrusions. Indeed when we mean by miracle an *intrusion* upon "natural law," we are unconsciously reproducing a major element in Mark's meaning for miracle, namely, intrusion upon the demonically fateful course of a world wandered from God's purposes. If the Call of the Four is Mark's first example of the kingdom's having drawn near, we should expect it to contain some such intrusion.

The Call of the Four (Mk. 1:16–20): Abandonment

Indeed, the Call of the Four does bespeak "intrusion." Jesus came upon Simon and Andrew while they were at their usual occupation—"casting a net in the sea; for they were fishermen." James and John were similarly occupied "in their boat mending the nets." Jesus' call to follow him interrupted all that; Jesus issued his invitation/command in the midst of all such everyday activity. Coming as it did, it forced the four fishermen to choose between discipleship and worldly business as usual. "Immediately," Simon and Andrew "left their nets." The abandoned nets of Simon and Andrew, and the forsaken father of James and John "in the boat with the hired servants" are eloquent symbols of the intrusiveness of the call to discipleship as the primary illustration of the disruptive way the kingdom draws near.

It is important to recognize the symbolic meaning of the abandoned tools of the workaday world. Almost all commentators recognize the ideal character of the Call of the Four.[5] This summons was intended to convey the brute facts about discipleship in as brief compass as possible. Accordingly, the Call of the Four cannot be taken as a literal model for any reader's call to discipleship nor a statement on the ultimate value of work for followers of Jesus. Therefore it cannot be a literal model for our response to the call to discipleship.[6] The story is more like a symbol containing the essential elements in the call to discipleship. This is what commentators mean by an ideal scene.

The symbolism is clear. The first essential element in discipleship is that it breaks the flow of our ordinary preoccupation. It interrupts our devotion to the business to which the world has called us, because the world's business, by apocalyptic definition, contradicts the purposes of the kingdom of God. This intrusive element in the call to discipleship confirms the tradition of American Protestantism, established during the first Awakenings, that each adult Protestant must be able to recount an experience of electing or saving grace to qualify for church membership. That experience set the saint off from the world. All baptized children of members were expected to confirm their baptism by the same distinguishing experience of grace. The Awakenings and the evangelistic campaigns were intended to mediate such distinguishing grace. Neither sane Puritans nor their evangelical descendants expected that a majority of the world's population would be called to discipleship.

Shortly after the Second Awakening, a subtle shift in the Protestant perception of the American world began to take place. From the beginning, American Protestants leaned more on the Old Testament for their interpretation of their new world than on the New Testament. The idea of America as the Promised Land blocked perception of the American Protestant experience as still part of the passing evil age of New Testament apocalyptic thought. So when the Protestant project to Christianize America seemed at first to be succeeding, one of the first casualties was the sense that this intrusive experience of election to discipleship was any longer necessary.

Horace Bushnell was the first apostle and founding father of this anti-apocalyptic view of America and of the smoother, more convenient experience of discipleship that naturally accompanies it. In 1835 he wrote, "What nation ever did as much in fifty years to soften the condition of man and prove the faith of the cross?"[7] It was a rhetorical question. At the end of the Civil War (of all times!), he supposed that the work of Christianity—that is, the Protestantizing of America—

was practically done. Given such a Protestant world, the experience of discipleship no longer needed to intrude. The time of the kingdom had become American Standard Time. Bushnell's new theory of discipleship became a keystone of public-party piety. A Protestant child ought to grow up in America not ever thinking of himself as anything but a Christian.[8]

This theory neatly dispensed with the first essential lesson of the Call of the Four and launched the American tradition of cheap grace. Bonhoeffer traced his heritage of cheap grace to Luther's contrasting a doctrine of "justification by faith alone" with obedient response interpreted as "works of the law." Americans have not rationalized their compromises with Reformation theology. It was simply obvious to them that America was a complete exception to God-contrary "worlds" of Europe and of the New Testament; the experience of the call to discipleship need not interrupt the projects of Americans.

The irony of party history is that eventually those in public party, in its social gospel and neo-orthodox phases, were the Protestants who first came to realize that America was not the kingdom of God. But they never updated their piety to match this fresh perception of the American world. If the American world needed to be changed, it follows logically that the Americans within that world also needed to be changed. The public party never confirmed that logic with a call for conversion. Consequently, their politics reflect the cost of discipleship, but their piety mirrors cheap grace.

The companion irony is that the private party kept the notion of disruptive discipleship while embracing America as though it were Christian in all of its economic, political, and imperialistic essentials. The private party's version of cheap grace is so careful to circumscribe the disruption in the call to discipleship that it intrudes only on the private world of personal morality. It is not by accident that "born-again" Christians find their commercial involvements undisturbed by the call to discipleship, whether their converts happen to publish pornography or program media for jiggle and violence.

It certainly belongs to discipleship to be personally honest, chaste, and generally upright. So were the Pharisees. So was the rich man who had kept the commandments from his youth (an early disciple of Bushnell?). So presumably were the four fishermen. But discipleship confined to the small world of personal morality is not an experience of the drawing near of the kingdom. When the scribe agreed with the superiority of the double commandment of love of God and neighbor, that alone did not make him a disciple: It left him "not *far* from the Kingdom of God" (Mk. 12:34). For all its vaunted biblical evangelicalism, private-party piety leaves its devotees outside the sphere of discipleship looking in. To strew the site of one's call to discipleship with the abandoned flea-market trivia of beer cans, theater tickets, and a stack of old *Playboy* magazines is hardly the equivalent of the sturdy artifacts of nets, boats, and a father's business. Not until our devotion to the projects the nets and boats represent has been interrupted has the call to discipleship been truly heard. I find it a contradiction to put the call to discipleship in terms that reinforce economic virtue.[9] The Call of the Four found them *busy* as did the call of Levi (Mk. 2:13, 14). The problem was not that they were not diligent; it was that they were diligent about the wrong things.

The key to the symbolic meaning of abandoned nets, boats, and parents is the realization that the "world" exercises its tyranny over us mostly at work and after that in families. If ever God is to break the world's domination of us and displace it with His own reign, it must be in connection with work and family.

How à propos the story of the Call of the Four is for American Protestants addicted to the Protestant ethic! It is so apt because the Judaism of Jesus' day had already pioneered the Protestant ethic. That ethic can easily be caught by a selective reading of the Old Testament. Remember Ben Franklin's favorite text from Proverbs? By Jesus' day, Judaism had concluded that a major mark of God's elect was wealth; so, to work hard and prosper was central to Jewish piety. This conventional wisdom was what made Jesus' comparison of rich men with excluded camels so astonishing to his followers (Mk. 10:25). Peter and those with him had assumed that riches were a sure mark of inclusion in the kingdom. When Jesus made riches an obstacle to eternal life, the disciples, still sharing the conventional wisdom, were thrown for a religious loop: "Then who can be saved?"

The answer of both the Call of the Four and the Call of Levi is that those can be saved who repent of their religious devotion to the world's work and who believe instead that following Jesus is the main business of life. Especially since the Gilded Age, American Protestants have assumed that pursuit of riches and following Jesus are not in conflict. Remember the famous exhortation of the Reverend Russell Conwell? "Get rich, get rich, get rich!" The stories of the call to discipleship simply dispose of that as the business of life.

Family runs a close second to work as a vehicle of the world's tyranny. We saw the connection between family and world in the last chapter. The family is the vehicle the world uses to get at our psyche and program it for worldly ends before we have the capacity to resist. Abandoned Zebedee, James's and John's father, is the symbol of the break that discipleship makes with the world on this front.

But neither work *per se* nor family itself is incompatible with discipleship; Jesus did not demand ascetic withdrawal from them. If we look for Jews in Jesus' day who followed this road out of the world, they were the Essenes at Qumran, not the disciples of Jesus. Peter's home remained intact after he became a disciple. His house in Capernaum became a refuge for Jesus and a base of operation for the mission. The abandoned boat turns up again as a platform from which Jesus taught the crowds on the shore and as transportation to and from the other side of the sea. Peter did not fish during Jesus' ministry because being with Jesus had become his work during that special period. Because Peter and others literally left their work to be with Jesus for a time, they reported to us what it was like to be with him. Because of their report, no one need ever quit working to be with him. Through their testimony, all who will may follow him—while they remain at work.

It is a central conviction of the Protestant adventure that work and family can and must be vehicles of discipleship. The subsequent use Jesus made of Peter's home and of the boat symbolize that. But the place of work and family within the context of discipleship unfolds only after the positive content of discipleship has taken effect. That positive content is given in the command, "Follow me."

Following Jesus

What the four left work and family *for* was to follow Jesus. "Follow me," Jesus said. And in each case "they followed him."

This is what discipleship is mainly about. The noun *discipleship* does not occur in Mark or in the New Testament. There are only forms of the verb *to follow*. The English word *disciple* comes from another root.

In each case the word links the activity of discipleship to the familiar world of Palestinian Judaism. The most obvious parallel to discipleship is the relation of student to rabbi. In this relationship the student literally "went behind" his teacher at a respectful distance wherever the master went. The words in the Greek text at 1:17, 20; and 8:34 put the action in this fashion, for example: "if any man would *come after* me...." Even with the simple Greek for *to follow*, the picture of action is the same—for example: "And those who went before and those who *followed* cried out, 'Hosanna! (11:9).

The pictorial aspect of following at a respectful distance only suggested the more important aspect of the relationship that the student had to the rabbi of his choice. What was more important was that the student or disciple followed in the sense that he left his own home and moved in with the rabbi to memorize his teaching and to observe the way the rabbi applied his teaching in action. The student stayed with the rabbi until he had mastered the body of law and interpretation. Then he left the rabbi to become a teacher on his own.

There are obvious parallels between the rabbinic model and Christian discipleship. Jesus' followers were also called "disciples"—the same word used for rabbinic students. In Hebrew the word for *teacher* and *student* come from the same root. Accordingly, in Mark *Teacher* is the most frequent title for Jesus used both by disciples and others. Four times his disciples use it (4:38; 9:38; 10:35; 13:1). Once, a scribe used it with respect, thereby granting Jesus rabbinic dignity (12:32). Opponents use it to flatter (12:14) and to propound a scholastic question (12:19). People in general use it (9:17; 10:17, 20). Jesus acted like a rabbi, teaching in public in the synagogue (1:21, 39; 6:1 ff.) and in the Temple (14:49). Three times he is actually addressed with the title "Rabbi": twice by Peter (9:5; 11:21) and once by Judas (14:45). One special time he is even called *Rabbouni*, a term of such deep respect that Judaism eventually restricted it to God (10:51). So in Mark, Jesus obviously appeared to be a rabbi with a following of students. Consequently, it is tempting to explain discipleship in this setting, at least from a formal point of view.

But if the comparison sheds light, it also baffles. John's disciples fasted, as did the disciples of the Pharisees, but Jesus' disciples did not (2:18 ff.). Rabbis were supposed to uphold the written law and its traditional oral interpretation. Jesus set aside kosher, distinctions of clean and unclean, and relativized Sabbath observance. Indeed, Jesus did not make Law the subject of his teaching at all; if he had a subject, it was the kingdom of God. But even then, there is little discourse in Mark that one could associate with a body of learning. Only chapter four has anything like a lecture on a theme. Chapter thirteen, the other discourse in the book, is an apocalyptic prophecy.

Other aspects of Jesus' relation to his disciples break the rabbinic mold. Prospective students applied for acceptance to their chosen rabbi. With Jesus it was the other way round: he called the disciples into the relationship. Also, Jesus placed demands on his followers beyond anything expected by a rabbi, such as forsaking the family as the basic unit of social loyalty and identity (3:31–35), divesting oneself of riches (10:21), and denying oneself to the point of accepting the prospect of one's death in service of Jesus rather than suffer final judgment at the end of the age (8:34–38). What is most striking is that although Jesus as a teacher had for his theme the kingdom of God, he called disciples to attachment to himself. "Follow *me*!" In fact Jesus made attachment to himself the way to entrance into the kingdom of God, putting himself in the place a rabbi would have given to Law (10:21).

From the point of view of subject matter, Jesus was closer to a prophet than a rabbi. Like John the Baptist and a line of prophetic figures in first-century Palestine, he announced the near end of this age and the dawn of the age to come. Usually such figures began to gather an eschatological-revolutionary movement that was then put down with utter ruthlessness by the Roman authorities. According to Mark, the crowd saw Jesus in these terms, as did Herod. (8:28; 6:14, 15)

The prophetic model does illumine the Call of the Four and of Levi. Indeed, the scheme common to them follows the pattern set in 1 Kings 19:16, 19–21 when Elijah called Elisha to be a disciple. "Just as God, Himself, called individual prophets away from work and family so Jesus called individuals away from all human involvements so that they might follow him."[10] That explains the stark demands for a break with the world in the forsaking of work and family. It also explains the positive side of discipleship as a service of the eschatological, apocalyptic, imminent kingdom of God. It explains as well how the disciples were called to participate in Jesus' ministry, until it reproduces itself in them. Elisha eventually received the mantle of Elijah's ministry and continued that movement. This is no doubt the meaning of the hint in the call of Simon and Andrew—"I shall make you become fishers of men."

Jesus chose twelve for this special task of sharing his ministry in chapter three and sent them on a mission in chapter six. But when that function was completed, Jesus continued to call disciples without regard to participation in his mission. After the return from their mission, the twelve blend more and more into a host of disciples who also received a call to discipleship. "And he called to him the multitude with his disciples and said to them, 'If any one would come after me....'" (8:34). The prophet model illumines the relationship of Jesus to the twelve but not to the host of other disciples Jesus made. Yet the prophet model breaks down in the face of the betrayal by the twelve and the forsaking by all at Jesus' arrest.

From the point of view of discipleship, this blanket failure of all of Jesus' disciples to keep faith with his movement is most puzzling. We know from the subsequent history of the early church that disciples of Jesus did recover from the tragedy of the crucifixion to continue the movement. The most distinguishing feature of the book of Mark compared to all other New Testament literature is that it provides no record of the recovery of disciples from their apostasy at the arrest. To be sure, the book clearly announces the resurrection. But the remarkable thing is that there is no record of the disciples' experience of it.

Even the resurrection announcement is curiously indirect. There is only an empty tomb and an "angel" with a message but no resurrected Christ. The announcement itself came not to the familiar "name" disciples but to a group of women. The women appear only at the end of the book in connection with the resurrection announcement, so that the author seems to have used them to avoid attributing any positive experience to Jesus' closest disciples that would compensate for their pell-mell defection. And strangest of all, the book closes with the notice that the women were so distraught that they did not deliver the message (16:8). As a consequence, the reader is left wondering what became of their commitment to follow Jesus. Was there any way for it to continue after Jesus' death?

Tradition and scholarship have worked out convenient responses to these puzzles. Two centuries later, scribes collated appearances of the risen Christ from the other gospels and added them to the book. This seemed to solve the problem of the failure of the women to report by giving the disciples their own experience of resurrection. That, of course, rehabilitated the original followers and accounted for the continuation of Jesus' movement. The fact that this addition is obviously not a part of the original book cancels out its value as a solution to the puzzle that the book itself raises. To argue that there must have been some such ending in the original work simply refuses to accept the problem that only the original version of the book poses. Before resorting to rewriting a work that puzzles us, surely we should first exhaust every other possibility.

One answer to the question of what became of the commitment to follow Jesus is that with the end of Jesus' earthly ministry, discipleship as a form of Christian devotion became obsolete. One cannot "follow" a risen Christus.[11] This seems to be confirmed by the fact that the word for *following* only occurs once outside the gospels, where it is a synonym for the apostles, who, because they had been companions of the earthly Jesus, had special authority in the church (Acts 14:4). This answer seems confirmed by the book of Acts, which replaced following Jesus with experiences of the Holy Spirit.

Disciples of the Risen Christ

The trouble with this answer is that it overlooks the fact that the editor of the Gospel of John does make *following* the mode of relating (John 21:19, 22) to the resurrected Christ. Moreover, it is generally agreed that within the body of the book of John the resurrected Christ is being portrayed under the guise of the Jesus of the earthly ministry so that the following theme portrayed is intended to be a description of Christian life with the resurrected Lord (John 1:43; 8:12; 10:4, 5, 27; 12:26). This view of discipleship came about as a result of the original author's shift of the emphasis of eternal life from the future into the present life of the church.

What usually prevents a "Johannine" answer to the riddle

of Mark's ending is the assumption that the author of John was capable of such theological subtlety while the author of Mark was a relatively simple editor of source materials. That estimate of Mark is changing with the rise of redaction criticism.[12] We now see that this author's editorial activity, like that of the authors of Matthew and Luke, was a technique expressive of a high degree of theological original- ity.[13] In fact, the redaction critical perspective suggests that only Luke intended to relegate the ministry of Jesus to the past.[14] There is a growing consensus that the author of Matthew intended that at least some incidents in his book are camouflaged offers to the church of experiences with the risen Christ under the guise of episodes with the historical Jesus.[15] With this fresh appreciation of Matthew, the word *following* becomes an especially important clue to the views of the church of Matthew not on the past ministry of Jesus but on its present experience of discipleship[16]; it suggests an explanation of the riddle of discipleship in Mark.

The best place to begin to apply this explanation is at the end of the book, where the riddle was most starkly posed. The book ends with the disciples having defected, but a promise of Jesus at the Last Supper—"after I am raised up, I will go before you to Galilee...." (14:28)—reinforces the message of the angel in the empty tomb, "go tell his disciples and Peter that he is going before you to Galilee; there you will see him" (16:7). Both verses are most probably creations of the editor.[17] The experience they promise offers the only possibility for restoration of the disciples and continuation of Jesus' movement. Commentators pose two possibilities for that experience. One is that the seeing of Jesus, to which reference is made, is the coming of Jesus as the Son of man promised in chapter thirteen.[18] The other is post-resurrec- tion appearances.[19] The first is ruled out by the nature of the *parousia* as it is described in chapter thirteen. There it is a cosmic event elevated above a flat world, simultaneously present to every earthly location (13:26,27). For such an event it does not matter where on earth one is, including Galilee.

The second explanation leads to the hypothesis of the lost ending. As I have suggested, this ought to be only a refuge of last resort when all the possibilities in the book as we have it have been exhausted. The second explanation has the advantage over the first in that it does deal with resurrection appearances. It seems clear in both 14:28 and 16:7 that the context is resurrection. And in connection with the theme of discipleship, only resurrection appearances of some kind could rehabilitate disciples who had fallen away. The difficulty of the conventional solution is that it supposes that the only kind of resurrection appearance available to Mark was the kind found in Matthew and Luke.[20] It is a natural extension of the redaction-critical estimate of the author of Mark to allow him greater creativity.

I find it suggestive to begin where the author began when he created the gospel form as a connected account of Jesus' ministry. Before that amazing creation there had been for the most part only disconnected stories about Jesus. In studying them, form critics rightly supposed that the original function of these isolated pieces had been to provide material for the proclamation and teaching of the early church ("I describe preaching as the original seat of all tradition about Jesus....").[21] In these stories used for proclamation and teaching, the church conveyed the living presence of the risen Christ. In other words, the stories about Jesus' ministry had been micro-occasions of the appearance of the resurrected One.

Given that preaching in the early church had as its purpose to represent the risen Christ as the bearer of salvation, we might expect a book built from preaching materials to continue that purpose. This representation of the risen Christ Dibelius called *epiphany*. Because Mark composed his book out of this epiphany material, Dibelius called it "a book of secret epiphanies."[22]

Bultmann, the other expert on the nature of pre-Marcan, pre-gospel materials, judged Dibelius's epiphany view of Mark as "just right."[23] He too recognized the continuity between the function of the building blocks of oral tradition and the final literary form Mark gave them. After emphasizing the preaching purpose behind Mark's arrangement of the oral materials into a literary composition, Bultmann made precisely the point I am emphasizing—namely, that the original building blocks of oral tradition and the written story of Jesus' ministry in Mark serve the same function.

> The process of literary history is in the last resort comprehensible only on the basis of the fundamental presupposition, that in all the sayings of Jesus which were reported, he speaks who is recognized in faith and worship as Messiah or Lord, and who, as the proclamation makes known his works and hands on his sayings, is actually present for the Church.[24]

The point I am making is that the early church preserved the tradition about Jesus for preaching and teaching because in it the risen Lord continued to make appearances. When Mark first composed a connected account of Jesus' ministry from the materials of this tradition, he had the same purpose in mind. The author of Mark composed his work as a vehicle for the appearances of the risen Jesus.

This conclusion is confirmed by the author's own description of his work. He chose to call it "the gospel" (1:1). In Marxsen's pioneering work on Mark, he included an essay on the use of this word.[25] He concluded that it was the author of Mark who first introduced this term into the materials of the Jesus tradition. By that time the meaning of the word *gospel* was well established in the early church. It meant the message about the life, death, and resurrection of Jesus the Christ, through which the living Lord offers salvation to those who believe. "In other words, Jesus is the content of the gospel; Jesus is present in the gospel; the gospel 'represents' him."[26] It is important in this connection to observe that although the author of the book called his work "the gospel," he did not mean by this a new literary form. It was indeed that, and it is natural that scholars should give it that designation. But for the author, *gospel* meant just what it had been meaning all along to the early church. What was new

was that the author now claimed that these materials from
the tradition about Jesus, when arranged into an account of
his ministry, could perform the same function that preaching
had previously performed. Of course the same response of
repentance and belief was required to make this form of the
gospel work (1:15 "repent and believe in the gospel").[27]

Mark's reason for placing no accounts of resurrection
appearances after the empty tomb was that he saw his whole
book as the place of encounter with the risen Jesus. The
message of the angel at the empty tomb to go to Galilee and
there see the risen Jesus was an invitation to the reader to
reread the book as the place of meeting the risen Christ.

This hypothesis accounts for the failure of the women to
convey the message to the disciples and Peter (16:8). The
author never intended the message for them; the message
was intended for the only ones who certainly do get it—the
readers of the book. The author showed in chapter thirteen
that he was perfectly capable of addressing the reader in the
guise of instructions to the disciples. ("Let the reader understand" [13:14].) I am suggesting that the author of Mark
expected the reader to understand that his book, as "gospel,"
served the function for readers that the traditional resurrection appearances had served for Jesus' original followers.

This explanation also makes sense of the puzzling designation of "Galilee" as the place of the appearances. Scholars
have never been able to reach consensus on the meaning of
Galilee as a geographical location in Mark.[28] One suggestion
is that it was the location for a Marcan church. This suggestion founders on the fact that the last location we can
discover for Mark's community is in Judea, not Galilee—"let
those who are in Judea..." (13:14). From there they were to
"flee to the mountains"—presumably Trans-Jordan. But the
final "location" of Mark's community would have been on the
move to all the nations of the earth where the gospel needed
to be preached before the Son of man should come (13:10). In
fact it may be misleading to think of the Marcan community
as a residential community at all, given the itinerant model of
Jesus' ministry and the discipleship connected with it. At

most, Mark's people were likely to have had no more than a home base analogous to the house of Peter in Capernaum.

If Galilee does not represent the location of a Marcan church, it is just as difficult to support its being the literal geographical location for the ministry of Jesus. All attempts to outline the Book of Mark on a geographical basis founder on the confusion this leads to. The Jesus of the book goes back and forth across the Sea and into the environs of Galilee in no plottable fashion. Two of the most significant revelatory events of the book take place outside Galilee—Peter's Confession at Caesarea-Philippi and the Transfiguration on a high mountain (Hermon?). But Jesus regularly returned to his Galilean base in Capernaum on the shore of the sea. And that is where in his own editorial summary the author has people come from the four corners of Palestine when they wish to see Jesus (3:7–8). The Galilean geography of the book makes the most sense when it is seen as a symbolic location from which Jesus launches his movement to all the nations. The message of the angel then invites the reader to return to the account of the ministry of Jesus, where it reads, "Now after John was arrested, Jesus came into Galilee preaching the gospel of God. . . ." (1:14). Only this time the reader is advised to look in the account for a resurrected, present Jesus, not a crucified and past one.

As Marxsen has pointed out, if the Marcan editor did intend his gospel to re-present the risen Christ, accounts of resurrection appearances at the end would have robbed all the events that went before of any resurrection function. "He (the author) proclaims the Risen Lord by means of stories from the earthly life of Jesus, and these would lose their character of direct proclamation if he gave an account of an event that was possible only after these had taken place."[29]

Rereading Mark as an Epiphany of the Risen Christ
THE MESSIANIC SECRET

Was the author of Mark capable of such subtlety? His so-called messianic secret and his doctrine of parables not only display such subtlety but they seem to fit well with this explanation of the end to the book. As Kee has observed, the true messianic secret in Mark is his intention to preserve Jesus' messianic identity within the circle of disciples (8:30 and 9:7).[30] The true identity of Jesus had to be confined within that circle because only when the crucifixion and resurrection had broken the patterns of conventional Jewish messianic expectation would Jesus' identity as Son of man make sense. The prevailing expectation was that the Jewish Messiah would come in the form of a charismatic warrior like David to free the Jewish people from the yoke of their Gentile oppressors. Jesus' career in Mark was the antithesis of such expectation; he died at the hands of the government a Davidic warrior was supposed to overthrow. Then how could Jesus be Messiah? He was, according to Mark, a Son-of-man Messiah whose work would climax not in the political event of a victorious holy war, but in an apocalyptic drama when he would return from heaven on clouds of glory at the end of the age (13:24–27).

According to the secret plan of God, he must first complete a career as an incognito messiah who would suffer, die, and rise from the dead. The mystery of who Jesus was in his earthly career was only revealed with his resurrection. But with that key, the believing reader could go back to Jesus' ministry and find in it already present the full benefits of post-resurrection salvation.

The secret identity of Jesus as the post-resurrection Son of man was given before the resurrection in the story of the Transfiguration.[31] The mandate not to relate the story until after the resurrection of the Son of man from the dead (9:9) shows that in offering the story within his book, the author has the permission that only came with resurrection. Likewise in 8:30 the caution not to reveal that Jesus is Messiah is immediately connected by the author to the suffering, death, and resurrection that will reveal Jesus as a Son-of-man kind of Messiah. The disciples could not, of course make sense of that at the time, but the author and reader who share the secret can relate to the Jesus of the ministry in his secret identity as Son of man in a way no historical companions could have.

Twice before sharing the secret in the predictions of the passion and resurrection, the author has offered glimpses of Jesus' true identity so that the reader could begin to relate Jesus' action and teaching to his Son-of-man identity. In 2:10 Jesus claimed that miracles of healing and forgiveness of sins amount to the same thing, and that he accomplished both by the Son of man's authority "on earth." The elements of the secret are all there: the authority of the Son of man—a figure who really belongs on clouds of glory in heaven—and a teacher-rabbi-prophet—a figure who belongs "on earth." By means of these historically incompatable identities the salvation of God is conveyed. This is the meaning of the complaint of bystanders. "Who can forgive sins but God alone?" (2:7).

The other cryptic notice of Jesus' identity was served on the reader in the incident of the upsetting of Sabbath observance. Jesus subordinated the claims of the Sabbath to the claims of human need with the pronouncement, "The sabbath was made for man, not man for the sabbath" (2:27). The authority for this pronouncement came from Jesus' secret identity—"so the Son of man is Lord even of the sabbath" (2:28).

Thus the author took advantage of the covert authority of the Son of man to meet two major fronts of Jesus' ministry— the miracles and the challenge to conventional Jewish piety.[32] Upon first reading it is difficult to imagine how these actions of Jesus exercising his authority as the Son of man could have made much sense. Upon rereading, in keeping with the directions from the empty tomb, they would help to highlight elements in Jesus' ministry especially significant as modes of the saving presence of the risen Christ. The saying at 2:10, "But that you may know that the Son of man has power on earth to forgive sins..." is Mark's designation of healing miracles as instances of the drawing near of the kingdom exactly parallel to the saying in Matthew and Luke, "And if I by the finger of God cast out demons, then the kingdom of God has come upon you." Within the perspective of the secret, the coming of the Son of man and the coming of the kingdom of God are the same thing (8:38ff; 9:1). Jesus'

challenge to Jewish piety involved not only Sabbath observance, but also the practices of fasting and keeping kosher
as well. Jewish piety had developed in part to preserve the
identity of the people of God by distinguishing them from
the aggressive world of Hellenistic culture. A break with
this piety would have meant a disorienting loss of identity
unless a new one were granted along with the break. For this
reason it was important for the author of Mark to allow
Jesus' identity to be known at this point so that the Son of
man could begin to bestow on the people of God the new
identity this crisis of piety called for.

THE PARABLES

The work of Wrede and the natural interest of churchly
scholars in Christology has given the "messianic secret" more
prominence than it perhaps deserves as a key to Mark's
intention. In my opinion a more important "secret" for
deciphering Mark has to do with parables. It was in connection with parables that the editor used the word "secret." "To
you has been given the secret of the kingdom of God, but for
those outside, everything is in parables" (4:11). This saying
occurs in one of three editorial passages that the author has
attached with explanation to a cluster of parables that were
his source.[33] The striking notion that ties the last two
summaries and two additional parables together is that the
parables function to conceal the truth. In the editor's view
parables are riddles that require divine explanation, otherwise they condemn the hearer to misunderstanding and
exclusion from salvation. In all historical probability, neither
Jesus nor the early church apart from Mark shared this
theory. Mark and his community borrowed the notion from
apocalyptic thought.[34]

Having grounded his view of parables on a special form of
Isaiah 6:9ff., the Marcan editor declared this notion to be
absolutely central to his presentation of the ministry of Jesus.
("... for those outside, everything is in parables" [4:11],
"... he did not speak to them without a parable" [4:34].)

These verses declare that the parable in the sense of a riddle was the *exclusive* means Jesus used to convey his message. That raises a problem: If we were to scan the book for parables, there are relatively few; most often Jesus seems to have taught *without* parables.

Research on parables in other apocalyptic literature in the milieu of Mark reveals that we would probably be looking for the wrong thing. In conventional language "parable" means some form of comparison, metaphor, or similitude. But apocalyptic literature of the time used a variety of forms and called them parables. Those forms included task or problem, vision, story, illustration, and poem.[35] This helps to explain why Mark often introduced Jesus in a teaching situation, but instead of the expected discourse, there follows a story of some action of Jesus. For example, Jesus' first session in a synagogue presents Jesus in a teaching role (1:21, 22) and closes with the audience reaction to the teaching (1:27). But instead of a lesson the editor relates an exorcism. The editor does this because the story of the exorcism was a "parable" in the sense that it revealed in a hidden way his gospel of the kingdom drawing near in the ministry of Jesus. With this realization that to the editor all accounts of Jesus' public activity are parables, we may now take the declarations of 4:11 and 4:34 at face value—"for those outside, *everything* is in parables" and "he did not speak to them without a parable."

Another element in Mark's notion of parable corresponds to the other literature in the apocalyptic stream. As we have seen, parable means riddle and many literary forms can function as parable. The final element in Mark's doctrine of parables is to supply a divine interpretation that makes it a means of revelation.[36] This too is a common device in apocalyptic literature. Mark found in his source the explanation of the parable of the soils. He used that as an occasion to convey his teaching that *each* parable of Jesus required a private explanation to his own disciples (4:34).

Mark, in common with other apocalyptic literature, viewed divine truth as a "secret" (4:11, 22), which only Jesus the divine messenger could explain. Thus the regular withdrawal of Jesus from the crowds for the purpose of private instruction to his disciples is his way of arranging the Jesus tradition to express his doctrine of parables.[37]

As followers of Jesus, the editor and his community continued to perform the same function of presenting and explaining divine secrets in their day as they supposed Jesus did in his. The two parables which the editor added in chapter four, in effect, commission him to continue this aspect of Jesus' ministry (Parable of the Lamp) and threaten him with loss of revelation if he does not (Parable of Measures). Indeed, the motivation for publication of his book can be explained by the sayings, "the measure you give will be the measure you get, and still more will be given you. For to him who has, will more be given..." (4:24, 25). For however cryptic the parabolic secret made the message of the kingdom in Jesus' day, the editor and his community were under commission to share that message openly and clearly in their day. To do so was the main meaning of their existence between the resurrection and the return of the Son of man (13:10). So in keeping with the intention of Jesus that "...nothing is hid except to be made manifest, nor is anything secret, except to come to light" (4:22), the editor wrote Mark to explain the meaning of the parabolic secret.

It follows that as Jesus and his messianic career are the content of gospel (1:14, 15) and that as that gospel is a secret, so the whole Book of Mark is at once a riddle and an explanation. Mark's doctrine of the parabolic secret, as much as any other consideration, grounds my hypothesis that the editor intended to offer the story of the Galilean ministry of Jesus as a riddle form of the presence of the resurrected Jesus.

Post-Resurrection Notes

Once this central secret of the book is out, the many hints to its post-resurrection location fall into place with full significance. We noted already the post-resurrection function of the Transfiguration (9:9). To these add the indications that the editor assumes a post-resurrection church in mission: casting out demons "in your name" (9:38); final rewards "be-

cause you bear the name of Christ" (9:41); editorial instructions to flee Judea in connection with the fall of Jerusalem
("let the reader understand") (13:14); designation of the story
of the anointing of Jesus at Bethany to accompany the mission to all nations (13:10)—"wherever the gospel is preached
in the whole world, what she has done will be told in memory
of her" (14:9); assurance to James and John that eventually
they will suffer martyrdom—"The cup that I drink, you will
drink; and with the baptism with which I am baptized you
will be baptized" (10:39); the delay of the Second Coming has
already been reckoned with—"there are some standing here
who will not taste death before they see the kingdom of God
come with power" (9:1); a churchly technique for healing
attributed to disciples in Jesus' day—"And they cast out many
demons, and anointed with oil many that were sick and
healed them" (6:13 Jas. 5:14); the editorial substitution of the
Lord's Supper for a Passover meal that implies the sacramental posture of the church (14:12–16; 14:17–25); obvious
parallels between experience of the church (13:9–13) and the
suffering of Jesus (chs. 14–16); and finally the promise by
John of the baptism in the Holy Spirit (1:8) finds fulfillment
in the exorcisms of Mark's church (9:38) and in the wording
of its witness under indictment (13:11). All these evidences of
a post-resurrection situation confirm the hypothesis that the
ministry of Jesus in Mark is only apparently the ministry of
the historical Jesus. The "historical Jesus" of Mark is a riddle
form of the resurrected Jesus. This is what makes the book
gospel.

A Jesus Available For Discipleship

As I hope to have demonstrated, Mark created the story of
Jesus' career precisely to make possible a following of the
resurrected Christ under the literary form of following the
Jesus of that career. It will enrich the resources of Christians
to include this way of describing Christian life along with
what has been an overwhelming preoccupation with the

"born-again" life of John and the "justified" life of Paul. Dietrich Bonhoeffer, the saint of neo-orthodoxy, has shown in *The Cost of Discipleship* how fruitful this neglected way can be. Here is additional justification for it in the intention of Mark.

I have taken such a long detour in the treatment of the call to discipleship because without a positive experience of the summoning Jesus there is no "compelling" reason to drop what one is doing should the call come. Everything depends on Jesus really being there for one to follow. The essence of discipleship is actually keeping company with *Jesus*. Being with Jesus, tapping the wellspring of his awesome and graceful presence, sharing the adventure of his mission— that is what makes the risk of abandoning nets, boats, and parents inviting. *He* is what makes discipleship worthwhile. This is why the words that describe the action of following Jesus often include prepositions that emphasize accompaniment—"[he] entered the house of Simon and Andrew *with* James and John" (1:29). "Jesus withdrew *with* his disciples..." (3:7), "...he got into the boat *with* his disciples" (8:10). "And suddenly looking around, they no longer saw anyone *with* them but Jesus only" (9:8).[38] At other times a preposition is used to emphasize the fact that discipleship means moving in with Jesus and sharing life with him. "And he appointed twelve to be *with* him" (3:14). "...the man who had been possessed with demons begged him that he might be *with* him" (5:18). "You also were *with* the Nazarene, Jesus" (14:67). In fact at 5:40, Peter, James, and John are simply "those *with* him." That is perhaps the briefest and most accurate way to describe what it means to be a Christian according to Mark.[39] In other instances the preposition of accompaniment is built into the verb of common action or a prefix. "And he allowed no one to *follow with* him except Peter, James, and John" (5:37).[40] Even when the word "follow" appears without a preposition to describe discipleship a dative of association is used. Every expression for discipleship underlines the "withness" of it.

Fishers of Men

Having decoded the parables of Jesus in his ministry and the discipleship that went with it, we may now decipher the hint of the original call of Peter and Andrew that they would be made "fishers of men" (1:17).[41] I think it extremely important to note that the metaphor "fishers of men" was used in the call to Peter and Andrew before they were commissioned for the particular temporary functions of preaching and healing. The call story is not a call to office but to discipleship, as the companion story of the call of Levi confirms.[42] Levi did not become one of the Twelve in Mark. It was Matthew who turned the calls of Peter and Levi into calls to apostolic office. Matthew accomplished this by making Levi one of the Twelve, by creating the churchly office for Peter, and by recommissioning eleven of the Twelve in a resurrection appearance (Matt. 28:16ff). In Mark, without those Matthean additions, the Twelve—including Peter—return from their mission to rejoin the rank and file of disciples to whom the balance of the book is addressed.

The appointment of the Twelve did imply that there was a special call to a prophetic function in the community of Mark. But it is very important to keep the traditions associated with "name" disciples in Mark from being diverted to create a clerical elite.

The "fisher of men" figure in the very first call served notice that the life purpose of all disciples is to become agents of the drawing near of the kingdom of God in the form of sharing life with Jesus, so that this experience of discipleship might reproduce itself in the lives of others. This now becomes the "business" of disciples. Mark used the phrase "fishers of men" because it was a direct play on the business at which the call found Peter and Andrew. The point is that discipleship cannot merely be added to the vocational preoccupations at which the call finds one. The real vocation, that is, central life purpose of a disciple, is to allow the movement of the nearing reign of God to reproduce itself through him or her—whatever may continue to be the disciple's method of earning a livelihood.

This meaning for "fishers of men" fits the interpretation of the parable of the soils. The "good soil" reproduces "thirty, sixty, and a hundredfold" (4:20). Responsive disciples who avoid the distractions of the cares of the world, delight in riches and the desire for other things (4:19), the precise accompaniments of business as usual, become channels for calling many others to discipleship. This unofficial function of discipleship appears throughout the book as the device by which the ministry of Jesus multiplied its effects. "And at once his fame spread everywhere throughout all the surrounding region of Galilee" (1:28). The word for fame has as its root the idea of hearing. Jesus' ministry spread by word of mouth. The spread of the effect of Jesus' ministry beyond Galilee into Palestine at large came by "hearing all that he did" (3:8).

Mark frequently pointed out how in particular cases people who were healed by Jesus spread the word of their healing, thus fulfilling the function of "fishers of men." The healed leper "... went out and began to proclaim much and to spread the word so that Jesus could no longer openly enter a town..." (1:45). As a result of the healed leper spreading the word, "people came to him (Jesus) from every quarter." The verse is a small summary that shows the hand of the editor. The words "preaching" and "the word" are technical terms for the missionary activity of the early church.

The Gerasene demoniac is an especially apt illustration of the responsibility of all disciples to be "fishers of men." The story of his healing closes with an editorial addition.[43] "After having been healed, he begged him (Jesus) that he might be with him," (5:18), that is, he wished to move in and to share life with Jesus in the literal sense of becoming a disciple. But Jesus forbade him and commissioned him instead to, "Go home to your friends and tell them how much the Lord (the risen Lord) has done for you...." At this point the author slipped into a post-resurrection designation for Jesus sweeping aside the parabolic veil that usually shrouded his ministry. Suddenly the risen Lord steps out of the story and directs the man in a post-resurrection setting. Now it becomes especially clear that the obedience of discipleship does not literally require leaving one's father, like James and John left Zebedee, but it can mean going home instead, when that serves the injunction to be "fishers of men."

What about this dimension of being "with Jesus"? In his healing, the ex-demoniac had already been with Jesus! Being "with" the risen Jesus does not mean withdrawal from common life into some clerical enclave, but taking the effects of healing and merciful experiences with the risen Lord into common life to share. "And he went away and began to proclaim in the Decapolis how much Jesus had done for him . . ." (5:20).

As noted above, the Greek word for proclaim is the one used by the church for its missionary proclamation. Indeed the substance of this verse is practically the same as the introductory summary of Jesus' message "preaching the gospel of God." (1:14). (Mark alluded to the responsibility to be "fishers of men" with the same expression, "began to proclaim," in the case of the healed leper at 1:45). By this editorial addition to the Gerasene story, Mark has turned the tradition of an incident in Jesus' ministry into a story of post-resurrection discipleship in which the parabolic Jesus of the ministry becomes the risen Lord who directs a disciple to the "fishing" responsibility which belongs to all discipleship. The phrase "and all men marveled" (5:20) indicates the effectiveness of his fishing.

The ex-demoniac's "preaching" was partially responsible for the bringing of the deaf man with a speech impediment to Jesus the next time he visited Decapolis (7:31ff). Again those who had brought the man "zealously proclaimed" (the same word for churchly preaching again) the news of his healing. At this point in the book, the fishing responsibility in conjunction with the ministry of Jesus had produced more response than he could handle, forcing Jesus to begin to avoid further public contact (7:24, 36). The author, having satisfied

himself that he has shown how disciples augment the ministry of Jesus with their fishing witness, now shifted emphasis
to the implication of the coming passion for discipleship. The
next chapter will deal with that aspect of discipleship. But
first we need to glance at one special version of fishing for
people.

Prophets vs. Disciples

The mission of the Twelve arose, in part, because Jesus
needed to augment his own ministry by authorizing certain
others to reproduce its essentials—preaching and exorcism
(3:14; 6:7ff). Choosing them for these particular reasons
added another call to the call to discipleship, a calling within a
calling. To that subsidiary calling Mark devoted only two
paragraphs, 3:13–19 and 6:7–13. We must respect that
modest emphasis by resisting the temptation to identify the
central four disciples with that subsidiary calling. For one
fleeting period they did function in it; but for the most part
they model discipleship for all and not for a specially commissioned few.[45]

With that reservation clearly in mind, it is accurate to say
that the Twelve during their brief mission reproduced Jesus'
ministry as prophet. As we have noted, Jesus fulfilled most
accurately the role of prophet. So when he chose some to aid
him in that function he was making them prophets as well.

The "sending out" paragraph begins with a Marcan creation (6:7) and closes with one (6:12, 13). The saying in 6:10 is
a Marcan insertion as the editorial phrase "And he said to
them" reveals. The return is also editorial (6:30). Teams of
two, not found in the parallel stories in Matthew and Luke,
remind us of early church missionary practice (I Cor. 9:6;
Acts 8:14; 15:36–40) and of the practice of John the Baptist
(Luke 7:19).

Mark's hand, the pairs of prophets, and the anointing with
oil all point to churchly practice. The exclusively Marcan
story of the unknown exorcist suggests that Mark's com-

munity continued to exorcise. The highlighting of prayer as a technique for exorcism confirms this (9:29; 11:24). But Mark clearly downplays the prophetic call within discipleship. Why?

The answer is to be found in Mark's experience with Christian prophets. For him they were a source of error, "False prophets will arise and show signs and wonders to lead astray, if possible, the elect" (13:22). With that experience in mind, the paragraph on procedures for prophets was probably defensive, laying conditions on them that would restrict their number to a minimum of exceptionally committed persons.

Then how would the gospel be preached to all nations if itinerant prophets tended to be unreliable? Mark's answer was simple—by means of his book! Mark was persuaded that a theologically correct tradition keeping alive the risen Jesus would serve the world mission better than the freewheeling itinerant prophets he knew. Moreover, circulation of his book would neither tax hospitality nor allow the message to be distorted by Zealot sympathizers.

Mark's unfortunate experience with prophets and his answer to it were a foreshadowing of the move the later church would make when, at the close of the second century, it created the New Testament canon to counter the excesses of the Montanist, charismatic prophets. Because of Mark's unfortunate experience with itinerant prophets, the selection and sending out of the Twelve probably deserve relatively little consideration in the exposition of Mark's discipleship theme.[46]

Four

The final element in the Call of the Four that is important for discipleship is the fact that more than one were called. If the heart of discipleship is being with Jesus, its sociological corrolary is disciples being with one another. Sometimes the company of disciples seemed to displace the family (3:33–35) compensating a hundredfold for loss of those relationships (10:29, 30). In fact the movement to which Mark belonged served to include elements of ordinary family life transposed into movement life. For example, the new converts were called "children" or "little ones," and parenting in terms of nurture in the movement became the counterpart of ordinary parenting.

Discipleship and Family

But the familial functions of the Marcan movement in no way suspended the ordinary family. If anything, compared to practices of either Jewish or Roman cultures (10:2–12), the Marcan teaching on marriage and divorce supported the family. Jesus was more affirming of the dignity of children than his own native culture (10:13–16). Sexual relations within marriage were part of the divine order which would only be superseded in the resurrection (12:25). While Mark's movement borrowed images from family and offered counterparts of family life experiences, it complemented family life. It was not out to compete with nor destroy the family.

Why then in Mark does the fellowship of disciples sometimes compete with the fellowship of family? The answer must be that some families opposed the commitments of discipleship. In these particular cases, the claims of discipleship override those of family. Mark portrays Jesus' own as being one such family (3:20–21; 31–35). And in Mark's own day many families opposed the commitments of the movement (13:12, 13). We need not suppose that that was necessarily or even usually the case. Jesus made Peter's home his base—mother-in-law and all. Levi entertained Jesus in his home (2:15–17), as did Simon, the leper (14:3–9). Families were hosts to the Twelve on their brief mission. The women who served Jesus in Galilee represented sympathetic families (15:40, 41). So in Mark there are more instances of families sympathetic to the claims of discipleship than opposed to them.

It is important to emphasize this congenial relationship between discipleship and family, otherwise renewed interest in a more serious discipleship among Protestants today might lead to shunting the Protestant adventure into outworn paths of withdrawal or semi-monasticism. The communal living patterns launched in the sixties still attract some radical evangelicals in the seventies. The unstated assumption of these experiments is that the nuclear family per se is an obstacle to discipleship. That assumption is not supported by Marcan data. In fact the vast majority of Americans do not now live in nuclear families. In contrast to the situation of the first century, the claims of Marcan discipleship are just as likely to challenge the anti-family, anti-marriage drift of American society as they are likely to call the claims of family into question. Indeed, a recovery of marital faithfulness like Mark mandates will be necessary if the family is to survive the pressure of modern American society. If discipleship in our time is interpreted as inimical to family life, that may be more a symptom of captivity to the spirit of our age than faithfulness to the spirit of discipleship.

Discipleship and Community

A similar capitulation to the spirit of our age may express itself in a wrongheaded understanding of community in Mark. A sociological approach to the study of the New Testament is now beginning to compensate for the long-standing neglect of this dimension of biblical scholarship. However, sociology, as a secular discipline, is likely to be insensitive to the dynamic center of Marcan community. I have claimed that experiences of the risen Jesus lie at the center of Marcan religion. In the measure that sociology remains secular, it lacks an adequate category for such a center; therefore, it tends to explain the Marcan community as one held together by memories of past experiences of Jesus and hopes for the future, both of which are coupled to an unfortunate present. The implication is that oppression, powerlessness, and alienation account for religious convictions about past and future.

Applied to Mark this leads to a picture of a community caught between the times, struggling to hold on until the advent of more favorable circumstances. Meanwhile, in the barren present, it is mainly sustained by its own commitment to wait. I submit that such a picture of the Marcan "community" is more a product of the limitations of sociology than of the record which that community has left. Just as historicism once disposed of the Jesus of Mark's gospel in simpleminded pursuit of "the historical Jesus," so now that same figure threatens to disappear into a community waiting for the new age. If the Marcan "community" had had no more contact with Jesus than sociology suggests, they would have all defected the movement long before any such community could have jelled.

Once it has been thoroughly established that the members of Mark's community thought of themselves first of all as people "with Jesus" and only then "with one another," we can see what they had to contribute to create a sense of community. Their contribution was embodied in their book. Essentially, their contribution to community was the creation of the story of the ministry of Jesus as a parable of their experience of the risen Christ in their midst. From a human point of view, what held them together was their conviction of the truth of that parable. Unless they continued to be "with Jesus," there was no compelling reason to continue to be with one another. Their book expressed this consensus that bound them together and was itself the vehicle of the central experience at the heart of that consensus. The center of the community and the book were tied together as grace is tied to means.

The Call and the Parties

The Call of the Four and the parallel Call of Levi included four elements important for discipleship. The first was the call away from the preoccupation which the world had assigned to them. For the fishermen, that was symbolized in the abandoned nets, boat, and in the case of James and John, their father Zebedee. The nets and boat, and in Levi's case, the seat of tax collecting, represent worldly business as usual. The call to discipleship as an experience of the drawing near of the kingdom of God necessarily interrupts that worldly business. The call, like the kingdom it serves, intrudes on this world and suspends commitments to its projects.

Hoge's research has revealed the fundamental preoccupation of contemporary Protestants to be an idolatrous commitment to family, career, and standard of living. I see these as an interlocking trio. The overarching goal is upward mobility and an ever-rising standard of living expressed in terms of continually increasing consumption of material goods and services. This requires a career that offers continually increasing income, preferably in types of work that also confer social status. Since the increased capacity to consume depends on income from career, career requires unconditional devotion. Family finds its place in the context of that unconditional devotion. Family must be willing to go to any lengths, suffer any hardship, bear any burden, move anywhere in order to sustain the breadwinner in his/her, or their, unconditioned commitment to career.

The family is also a school where the rising generation learns how to escalate its consumption while preparing to enter a career which will sustain this escalating consumption. The curriculum of this school involves a delicate balance and continual monitoring of the ways in which energy is expended. If the rising generation uses too much energy in consumption, it will fail in its preparation to enter a career that can support its escalating tastes. On the other hand, if it does not enjoy escalating consumption it may lose the motivation for the grinding preparation that a really promising career calls for. The discipline of balance calls for highly skillful parenting. The family commitments to career support and consumption are themselves often too demanding in terms of time and psychic energy, especially when both parents are engaged in careers. Too little energy is left over for nurture. Then a family finds its various commitments competitive and self-defeating.

Typically, the nurturing function is the function that suffers. The children, through parental neglect or ineptitude, lose their chance to get a firm footing on the escalator of career. The results are tragic. The rising generation has acquired the tastes for increased consumption without the career skills to sustain those tastes. Everyone is understandably disappointed, frustrated, and angry.

Even a very brief and general description of this interlocking trio of value commitments indicates just how total is the preoccupation it brings with it. It is this Protestant preoccupation that Jesus' call to discipleship intends to break. I cannot imagine Mark selecting more appropriate stories for Protestants—we are so famous for our peculiar commitment to work that our syndrome is called "the Protestant ethic."[47] Jesus came to them at work. Jesus comes to us at work. To break with the world, to face toward Jesus and the kingdom of God, to repent, means to make the break there.

The pieties of both parties tend to obscure this fundamental element in the call to discipleship. The private party since the Gilded Age has declared that work in America and the attendant pursuit of a higher standard of living are God's will for us. So increasingly, since the middle of the last century, Protestant evangelists in what became the private party tradition have merely added religious experiences to the worldly preoccupations of work and called it discipleship.

In 1915, Billy Sunday said, "There are thousands of honest, hard-working Americans who will not have to change much to become Christians." Protestants have tended to agree with him ever since. The result has been that American Protestants who took the trouble to have an experience of entrance into the Christian life find themselves never getting much further in discipleship, nor allowing the experience to make much difference in their ongoing lives. To borrow a comment of George MacLeod of Iona to Billy Graham, such "... religion never gets beyond the garden gate and that's why it's a monument to irrelevance."[48] This is the typical American Protestant version of cheap grace. We attempt to leave our

American world and our commitments to it in place while we sanctify those commitments with an "evangelical" experience.

No *evangelical* experience is possible under these circumstances—not according to Mark's evangel. The typical American evangelical experience leads not to discipleship but to delusion. The true call of Jesus first disentangles us from the world of work, then it invites us to be with him. For private-party Protestants to recover true discipleship they will have to peel back about a century of American evangelism. Private-party members need to make explicit that the call to discipleship begins in connection with work, for just as Jews did in Jesus' day we tend to lose our souls on the way to work. Most private-party members are still oblivious to the collision course between work and discipleship. Indeed they continue to pursue and propagate the party line that in America one need not worry about the world of work to be fully Christian.

In other decades the public party has been alert to the contrast between the world of work and the requirements of discipleship. The public party began in protest against the injustices accompanying the accelerated industrialization of America. Reinhold Neibuhr's early career was pastor-prophet to the industrial worker. The theology of justice had its roots in a critique of American economic arrangements, especially as these arrangements affected the industrial worker. With the rise of Fascism in Europe prior to World War II, public-party attention shifted to politics. Neo-orthodoxy in America arose as a theology of politics. The puzzling capacity of the New Deal to meet the dilemma and aftermath of the Great Depression without benefit of clergy or theology no doubt contributed to disenchantment with economics. The more blatant forms of evil that political Fascism threw up captured the attention of public-party prophets.

While the study of social ethics by the public party specialized in politics, theology of work did continue to receive some attention. The Federal Council of Churches launched a study in 1949 on Christian Ethics and Economic Life under a grant from the Rockefeller Foundation, which eventually produced six volumes. A World Council of Churches study on a Christian doctrine of work and vocation led' to *Work and Vocation: A Christian Discussion* published in 1954, the contribution of the U.S.A. study committee.

These studies had little to contribute to the concrete practice of discipleship at work because they were too comfortable with the world of work. As we have observed, New Testament discipleship is set in the context of an apocalyptic world view that distinguishes sharply between the kingdom of God and the world. Public-party theology typically does not make this sharp distinction. It often settles for a world where some measure of progress in social justice increasingly qualifies the world to be the kingdom of God. Such a sanguine view of the world blurs the boundary between discipleship and ordinary work in the world and leaves the Protestant extremely vulnerable to domination by the world through work.

Fishers of Men and Women

The culminating lesson about work taught by the call to discipleship is that followers of Jesus go to work primarily to be agents of the approaching kingdom of God rather than as servants of a career that promises a higher standard of living. True success at work, in discipleship terms, depends on the "catch", that is, on the degree to which others hear the call to discipleship at work. "I will make you fishers of men and women," may be defined as the calling to multiply the "kingdom effect" on and around the work site through the prayerful witness and action of the disciple. "Those who were sown upon the good soil are the ones who hear the world and accept it and bear fruit, thirtyfold and sixtyfold and a hundredfold."

What about the goods and services that are produced at work? Is not work adequately justified by the life-sustaining and life-enriching goods and services which it does produce?

Discipleship can give only a qualified, "Yes." The world arranges work not solely because it serves human needs but also because it serves the greed and pride of those who do the work. "For all that is in the world, the lust of the flesh and the lust of the eyes and the pride of life, is not of the Father but is of the world" (1 John 2:16). The products of the world's work do sustain life but in the process the world exaggerates its role. As the world offers a bite of its apple, it is with the seductive suggestion that this apple came exclusively from this world's tree of life. From discipleship's estimate of the world, the fact that it does provide for real human needs in the midst of so much effort to the contrary points to the mysterious grace of God who overrules an unruly world for our good. So the disciple prays to *God* for daily bread and gives thanks to *God* when it appears, although apparently the hand that serves it is the world's. So, while the disciple does some of the world's work for some of its product's sake, the disciple knows what the world does not know, namely, that we do not live by any of these products alone.

What a relief! This attitude rids work of its idolatrous pretention to do for us what only God can do. It relieves the Protestant ethic of its sanctimonious solemnity and replaces it with the playful expectation that by the mystery of God's grace, even Ma Bell may occasionally give us a break from her role as America's Jewish Mother by granting us her services without exacting too much from us in exchange. It is as though God engages the world of work with the left hand only, leaving the right hand free for the kingdom. And so it must be for the disciple—with all due apology to the left-handed among us.

In summary, the meaning of the abandoned nets suggests an alternative to the Protestant ethic. The ultimate work of discipleship is to become "fishers of men and women." Perhaps devotion to this work should be called the "discipleship ethic." It is the true Protestant ethic.

It is significant that Jesus borrowed the image for the work of the kingdom from the worldly work at which he found the Four. This suggests that ordinary work in the world is a parable of the work of discipleship. While on the surface servants of the kingdom may appear to be doctors, lawyers, Indian chiefs, that is only their cover. Their true identity is disciples of Jesus. Their true work is handling the nets of the kingdom.

·8·

Discipleship in Political Perspective

Mark's Setting for Discipleship

In order to see where the risen Jesus was leading the Marcan community, we need to recover the specific situation out of which the book was written. Once that situation is exposed, we will be able to see how the risen Jesus was going before them in the symbolic Galilee, the place where the risen Christ still leads disciples.

The style of one particular chapter in the book tips the author's hand. If the parabolic gospel form under which the author is writing calls for a description of the ministry of Jesus as though it were in the past, and yet the author wishes to describe his own present, the obvious editorial solution would be to have Jesus deliver a prophecy of the future. That prophecy would then become the editor's way of describing his own present. This editorial device of presenting one's present situation in the form of a prophecy from the past is so common in apocalyptic literature that most apocalyptic literature can be dated in connection with such prophecies. The editor seldom stopped with a description of his own present. He used the same prophecy to describe a future which was still unknown to him. That part of the prophecy was not likely to be an accurate description of what really unfolded in history. So the date of the writing of the prophecy will be the same as that of the last actual historical event which the prophecy described (under the guise of prediction) before it trailed off into historically inaccurate predictions and/or speculation about the heavenly drama of the End.

If we look in Mark for such a description of the future, it is unmistakably chapter thirteen. On critical analysis, the supposed prophecy of Jesus turns out to be just what we would expect—a composition of the editor.[1]

The editorial occasion for the prophecy is an exchange between Jesus and "one of the disciples" about the temple. In the temple cleansing incident, the editor has already declared the temple obsolete because Judaism refused to allow it to become a base for prayerful support of the gentile mission (11:17). The condemnation of the temple was reinforced by sandwiching the story of the cleansing of the temple within the miracle of the cursing of the fig tree. Mark's final stroke against the temple was the divine judgment at the crucifixion, which destroyed the curtain marking off the holy of holies. Tearing it from top to bottom symbolized God's abandonment of it as his dwelling place (15:38). This Marcan stance toward the temple ran afoul of a traditional saying of Jesus to the effect that after the destruction of the temple, Jesus would rebuild it. John accepted this as an authentic saying of Jesus (John 2:19), as did Matthew (Mt. 26:61), at least to the extent that he allowed two witnesses to agree to it. Mark, however, maintained that it was a false tradition on which no two witnesses could agree (15:59).

Having rejected that tradition, Mark needed to declare where Jesus had really stood on the future of the temple. Mark offered the exchange between a disciple and Jesus to set the record straight. Jesus had indeed declared that the temple would be destroyed, *but not that it would ever be rebuilt* (13:1, 2).[2] This, according to Mark, was the true public teaching of Jesus on the fate of the temple. In keeping with the editor's usual device, the public teaching is a riddle which must be explained privately. So Mark changes venue from the temple site to the Mount of Olives where the saying is explained to the four who carry the privileged insights of the Marcan community (13:3ff).

The Maccabean Parallel

Even without the private explanation, Mark, as we have seen, had already made a powerful statement. To threaten the temple was to threaten the very existence of Judaism. That was why Jesus' word about the temple was at the heart of the proceedings against him at the hearing before the Sanhedrin (15:53–59) and the theme of mocking at the cross (15:29, 30). Whenever the temple was threatened, all Judaism rose up in its defense. After the Maccabean Revolt, following the desecration of the temple by Antiochus Epiphanes in 168 B.C., the first fruit of victory was to restore the temple in 165 B.C. The book of Daniel was written at this time.

When we turn Jesus'private explanation to the four, two features of the Maccabean experience are present—the profanation of the temple and war. Verse 14 borrowed the very terms Daniel used to describe the profanation of the temple —the "desolating sacrilege" (Dan. 11:31). The militant response described in terms of sword, flame, captivity, and plunder (Dan. 11:32–35) find their parallel in Mark's description of war and its attendant chaos (13:7–8; 14–20). If we look for an event in the period of the writing of Mark's gospel that corresponded to the Maccabean experience, the obvious one is the Jewish revolt against Rome which began in Jerusalem in 66 A.D. and ended with the destruction of the temple in 70 A.D. This is the event by which we date the prophecy. In connection with this event, we discover the difficulties in which the Marcan community found itself at the time its thoughts jelled into a book. The book of Mark was composed sometime during the war of the Jews against Rome and the author and his community fled into trans-Jordan before the final victory of the Romans in 70 A.D. that brought with it the destruction of Jerusalem and the temple.

A significant difference between this war and the one fought by the Maccabees was that it began at the initiative of the Jews. But the wars were very much alike in that they both triggered expectation that the final drama had begun through which God would fulfill his promises of salvation to his people. The Zealot party within Judaism had begun the war in keeping with their understanding of that drama. Their scenario revolved around the idea of a holy war in which a charismatic warrior like David would arise leading God's people to victory over the Gentiles after which the Jewish nation would stand proud before all the nations of the earth.

The idea of a holy war under Jahweh was as old as the conquest of Canaan. It was very much alive in New Testament times both in the Zealot party and in the Qumran preparation for the War of the Sons of Light against the Sons of Darkness. The Zealot version of the End was the one held by Mark's opponents. This version of the drama of the end time depended on direct military action and played itself out on the stage of history.

Daniel's Version of the End

Another version of the final drama developed among Jews in connection with the rise of the apocalyptic view of history. Daniel represents the beginning of this version. According to it, the goal of history is a kingdom of God beyond history. Daniel made allowance for a stormy military prelude which he interpreted as the birth pangs of the future age. But the future age itself would come only with an all-powerful intrusion of God and not through the initiative of a warrior people and their messianic leader engaged in a holy war. As far as Daniel was concerned, the efforts of the Maccabees were merely "a little help" (Dan. 11:34). Finally, everything would depend on an apocalyptic act of God interrupting ordinary history.

In the first century of the Christian era, Jewish expectation of the near approach of the final drama had intensified. Jesus had been preceded by a string of pretenders to the role of prophetic or messianic agent who claimed to announce or inaugurate the final drama. The Teacher of Righteousness who founded the Qumran community belonged to this line as did the Zealot leaders who launched the war against Rome in Mark's day. But in Mark's day, just as in the days of Daniel and the Maccabees, there were two very different scripts for the expected drama. Like the Maccabees, the Zealots had begun their revolt following a holy war script for that drama in which military action would lead to victory for the Jewish nation and fulfillment of their destiny on the stage of history. Like Daniel, Mark and his community were convinced that the End could only come by divine intervention and fulfillment in an age of resurrection beyond history. The difference between these two versions of the end drama accounts for the special posture Mark's community adopted in its situation.

It is important to remind ourselves that in Mark's day the followers of Jesus were still a sect within Judaism. Christianity as a religion separate from Judaism had not yet developed. So Marcan disciples of Jesus were as greatly stimulated by the eschatological connotations of the Zealot war as were other Palestinian Jews. The expectation of an immediate end to history which dominated the movement in Jesus' day must have been rekindled by the war. But their apocalyptic version of the kingdom of God and its accompanying Son-of-man christology convinced the Marcan community that the war was not God's way to the End. It was at most an unfortunate prelude.

Marcan Resistance to the War

According to the Marcan script for the eschatological drama, the End could only come with the arrival of the Son of man from heaven. Consequently, Mark's people refused to participate in the war and rejected the messianic claims of its leaders even if losing the war should lead to the destruction of the temple. Indeed, convinced as they were that this was not God's war, they knew that the effort was bound to fail and that along with that failure, the temple was sure to be destroyed.

Marcan Jews were not the only ones who opposed the war. After all, Zealots were only one party within Judaism.

Pharisaic politics called for cooperation with Rome, and the Qumran community had its own special version of the End. Still, the Zealots had captured public opinion. At the beginning, the war had gone very well. Josephus, tells us that after an abortive attempt of the Romans to put down the revolt, there was little opposition to the revolt left among Jews in Judea.³ It was a time when Zealot advocates of war pressed pacifist Jews to make a revolutionary stand. Chapter thirteen contains the record of Mark's reasons for refusing to succumb to that pressure, and of the price his community paid for dissent.

Zealot pressure on the Marcan community was no doubt exacerbated by the fact that some followers of Jesus shared the Zealot ideology, giving it a Christian twist. Mark began his rebuttal by conceding, in the form of prediction, that Zealot Christians were having an effect within his community. "Many will come in my name" (13:6) refers to these fellow disciples. The seeming prediction "they will lead many astray" becomes in our method of interpreting retrospective prophecy, a description of the effect they were actually having in Mark's time.

Mark's opponents were claiming that the successful leaders of the war were the returning Christ doing the second time what Jesus had failed to do as Messiah the first time (13:6, 21, 22). That claim was reinforced by miracles (13:22) as well as by the apparent success of the war. Over against this political, charismatic warrior, Mark offered a heavenly Son of man coming on clouds of glory to gather the elect—a figure calculated to contrast starkly with any competing earthly figure (13:24–27). This gathering of the elect by the Son of man replaced war as the vehicle of the End. The war had a place in the divine scheme, but only as an unfortunate prelude (13:72).

Mark's apocalyptic politics put him in the most difficult position imaginable. Fellow disciples of Jesus had developed a christological justification for the war, so that Mark's community was opposed from within the Christian community. Zealot politics had swept Palestine so they were opposed by non-Christian Jews as well. In wartime, all communities define opposition to war as treason and impose the death penalty. The section of chapter thirteen which describes the experiences of Mark's community shows every evidence that accusations of treason and the consquent death penalty were being imposed on Mark's community (13:9–13). Most distressing to Mark's people was the way their own families (and fellow sectarians?) felt it their duty to turn them in as traitors and subversives (13:12).

Having rejected the holy war of the Jews, Mark's only other possible political refuge was the Romans. Johanan ben Zakkai, leader of the postwar Pharisaic renaissance, escaped during the war to make a deal with Rome. Josephus, the Jewish historian of the period, had also accepted Roman hospitality in return for loyalist propaganda. But Mark's apocalyptic politics made him as unacceptable to Romans as he was to Zealots. To Zealots, he was a subversive pacifist. To Romans, he seemed an incorrigible revolutionary, committed as he was to an immediate end of this age under the auspices of a returning Jewish Messiah. One could hardly expect a Roman judge to catch the distinction between a son-of-David Messiah and a Son-of-man Messiah. So Marcan disciples were hauled into Roman courts before governors and kings where they fared no better than before Jewish councils and in synagogues (13:9). In such a completely hostile climate, no wonder they felt "hated by all" (13:13).

Jesus: Model for Suffering Discipleship

They were able to maintain their poise in this excruciating squeeze because their version of the End accommodated the war, and because their version of Jesus' ministry showed them how to conduct themselves under this persecution. Since Daniel, apocalyptists accepted the idea of a period of social chaos, natural catastrophe, and war as a prelude to the final act in the drama of the End (Dan. 11; 12:1ff). Accordingly, Mark was able to include the turmoil of the war against

Rome within the events associated with the End (13:7–8; 15–23). But he was careful to make the point that they were only preliminaries—"but the end is not yet" (13:7), and "this is but the beginning of the suffering" (13:8). This robbed the revolt of the ultimate significance the Zealots gave it. Still, the fact of the revolt and the persecution it brought were acceptable to the Marcan community since in the divine plan "this must take place" (13:7). Within this necessity, God had set a limit to the chaos so that it would not be allowed to overwhelm the faithful—"for the sake of the elect . . . he shortened the days" (13:20).

The necessity for suffering was for Mark not just a fateful by-product of a generalized apocalyptic point of view. Mark's account of Jesus' ministry had taught his community that suffering and discipleship belonged together. It had been a divine necessity in Jesus' career, and those who followed him had to reckon with that same necessity for themselves. Mark used the same term, "it is necessary," for suffering in Jesus' career as well as for the war. Moreover, Scripture even pinpointed particular events in the inevitable divine plan.

The passion narrative is woven on the warp and woof of divine necessity and scriptural fulfillment. The first prediction of the passion reads, "*it is necessary* for the Son of man to suffer many things . . ." (8:31). The conversation following the Transfiguration alludes to the scriptural ground for the suffering: ". . . and how is it written of the Son of man that he should suffer many things and be treated with contempt?" (9:12).

Having grounded the suffering of the Son of man in divine necessity and Scripture, the editor composed two more predictions of the passion of the Son of man (9:31; 10:33). They borrow their authority from the double ground of "it is necessary" and Scripture.[4] The divine plan revealed in Scripture enabled Jesus to forsee his arrest —"let the scriptures be fulfilled" (14:49)—and the betrayal of the disciples —"You will all fall away, for it is written, 'I will strike the shepherd and the sheep will be scattered'" (14:27). So the elect of Mark's community endured the trials and persecutions of their time in the assurance that God was in control of these events just as He had been in control of comparable events in Jesus' ministry.

But there is a crucial difference between discipleship in Mark's time and discipleship during Jesus' ministry. Mark fully expected readers of his gospel to endure the suffering that accompanies discipleship, while the original followers of Jesus all forsook him and fled. What made the difference?

The answer has to do with the politics of discipleship. This is not immediately clear in Mark's description of the failure of the original disciples. They seem to be excused by the necessity of the divine plan revealed in Scripture (14:27). Yet they are to be held responsible for any defection at the time the Son of man returns in glory (8:38). Some of them did recover their status as disciples and go on to accept the martyrdom they refused to share with Jesus. Mark knew at least of James and John (10:39). So it seems that Mark was saying that, while the first disciples were excused for their defection in Jesus' lifetime because of divine necessity, they and all subsequent disciples must do better, even at risk of martyrdom.

The point of Mark's portrayal of the archtypical disciples is neither to excuse nor to condemn them. It is to expose the particular misunderstanding that led to their defection so that disciples in Mark's time need not continue the same misconception.

The crucial misunderstanding comes to the fore in connection with each prediction of the passion of Jesus. This is precisely where we would expect to find it. The three predictions of the passion are creations of the editor.[5] Since Jesus' suffering is partly a model for discipleship, the editor coupled the lesson of suffering and discipleship to them.

The first prediction occurs in the conversation at Caesarea-Philippi (8:27–33).[6] It follows the confession of Peter, speaking for the disciples—"Who do you (plural) say that I am?", at which point the disciples identified Jesus as Messiah and not merely the prophet of popular opinion. The striking difference between Peter's confession and the passion prediction that follows is in the christological titles. Peter used "Messiah" but the passion prediction uses "Son of man." Peter objected to the passion prediction exposing the fact that "Messiah" for him did not include suffering and death. However, for the editor, suffering and death were inevitable for the Son of man. Each passion announcement uses Son of man. By the shift of titles, the editor declared that an understanding of the place of suffering hinges on the difference between a "Messiah" christology and a "Son of man" christology. Peter's failure to catch the difference put him on the side of Satan against God (8:33).

The editor made no further comment on the nature of the misunderstanding beyond the shift in title from "Messiah" to "Son of man." But that is enough to set us on the track. "Messiah," in popular Jewish expectation, meant a charismatic warrior in the style of David who would lead the nation of Israel to victory over the Gentiles. "Messiah" was the key title for Zealot politics.

On the other hand, the title "Son of man" demands a completely different field of reference. Instead of political victory on the plane of history, the politics of the Son of man transfers vindication to a heavenly stage beyond history. Where Zealot, Messiah politics expects military victory in holy war followed by political supremacy, Son of man politics expects death and resurrection, followed by a heavenly kingdom.

The implication of Son of man politics for discipleship is that so long as followers of Jesus remain on the historical stage, they are fated to suffer like the Son of man. This is what Peter could not have understood. The relationship between christology and discipleship explains why Mark created the pattern which he followed in each of the three passion predictions—first, predictions of passion, then misunderstanding, and finally, the corrected version of discipleship.

The corrected version of discipleship repairs the mistaken christology. For example, in the teaching on discipleship at Caesarea-Philippi, each correct statement about discipleship posits the mistaken version that goes with a Davidic, Zealot politics. Denying oneself and taking up of the cross contrast with self-fulfillment and victory in Zealot discipleship (8:34). The Zealot disciple aims to save his life (8:35) and gain the whole (gentile) world (8:36) by means of the holy war. To speak of self-denial, cross, and loss of the world are shameful (8:38) to Zealot sensibilities.

The editor repeated the same pattern in the second prediction. First, there is the prediction: arrest, death, and resurrection—using the Son of man title (9:31). Then the disciples fail to understand (9:32). This time, Peter has no special prominence. We must not suppose that misunderstanding of passion and discipleship was more of a problem for Peter than the others. When Peter spoke at Caesarea-Philippi, it was for the others. "Who do *you* (plural) say I am? Peter answered... And he charged *them* to tell no one about him" (8:29–31).

Correction for discipleship comes in the following episode where the disciples have been discussing who was the greatest among them (9:33–37). Zealot politics calls for domination of outsiders and status according to rank within the victorious people of God. The spoils of victory and relative status of the victorious are all to be distributed according to rank. Hence the question of who is the greatest. The politics of the Son of man turns the conventional political order upside-down. In that order, the slave of all has highest status (9:35). It is not immediately apparent here how suffering and servanthood are linked. Mark returned to clarify that connection in the third prediction.

Here again we meet the same pattern. There is the prediction of passion of the Son of man, this time with two additional elements. The suffering is specifically connected with the journey to Jerusalem (10:32–33). The suffering is at the hands of the Gentiles (10:33). This is calculated 'o contrast with Zealot politics in which the Gentiles are ᴧe ones who suffer. The approach to Jerusalem heightened the Zealot expectation of Jesus' followers, for it was to be the seat of the future revolutionary government and the place where the holy war was to begin. These were both realities in the Jerusalem of Mark's day. In 66 A.D., the Zealots began the war by taking the strongholds of Jerusalem by surprise and ran the war from a Jerusalem liberated from gentile domination.

In the third prediction, Mark did not repeat the misunderstanding of the disciples explicitly but described them as amazed and afraid (10:32), symptoms of misunderstanding. The specific misunderstanding with its correction follows in the request of James and John "to sit, one at your right hand and one at your left, in your glory" (10:37). Positions to the right and left of an important person designate rank of second and third place.[7] Sitting implies enthronement as in the case of Psalms 110:1 quoted at 12:36. The key to interpreting the request turns on deciding which enthronement James and John had in mind. The choice is between the enthronement of the exalted Son of man in heaven and the kingly majesty of a Davidic Messiah. Everything we have gathered so far about the disciples' grasp of their future with Jesus points to their meaning to share a Davidic enthronement with Jesus following the holy war which they expected Jesus was about to trigger in Jerusalem. The word "glory" has royal splendor of an earthly king as one of its meanings.[8] The reign of Simon in Maccabean times was described with just this word, which reign was an exact prototype of the disciples' political expectation.[9]

Satan uses the glory of national politics to tempt Jesus in Matthew and Luke: "... the devil showed him all the kingdoms of the world and the glory of them" (Matt. 4:8). "To you I will give all this authority and their glory..." (Lu. 4:5). It was precisely this temptation to which James and John had succumbed, along with their fellow disciples. Because they made their request in terms of Davidic politics, Jesus replied, "You do not know what you are asking" (10:38). When Jesus went on to answer in terms of the Son of man politics, they did not yet understand. There will be places at Jesus' right and left when he is enthroned as Son of man in heaven (v. 40), but they are reserved in the secret counsel of God for those who are willing to share the suffering (cup and baptism) discipleship requires (vs. 38, 40). James and John say they are ready to share the suffering of Jesus (v. 39). But the suffering they are ready for is the risk of becoming casualties in the holy war. Jesus continued his reply to the whole group of disciples in terms of concession to their misunderstanding by contrasting the domineering political style of Gentiles with the style of Son of man which achieves status by service. Finally, the climactic statement for the Son of man political style grounds that style in the suffering death of Jesus as Son of man (10:45). Mark did not have Jesus deny the ambition of disciples to achieve positions of status in the future. He did declare that Davidic politics is not the way to them.

This teaching on suffering, apocalyptic politics, was not understood by the disciples. They finished their time with him acting out a Davidic politics. When Jesus predicted the defection of all the disciples, Peter declared that he would remain faithful. His pledge was made on the basis of his readiness to engage in the holy war. Accordingly, when Jesus was approached to be arrested, the arresting body came with weapons to subdue Zealots ready to fight. One of the disciples, thinking the time to fight had come, "drew his sword, and struck the slave of the high priest and cut off his ear" (14:47). That was the act of a Davidic freedom fighter in the best tradition of the Maccabees. No matter that the first casualty was a fellow Jew. Mattathias had begun his holy war by striking down "sinners" and "lawless men" among his own people before engaging the Gentiles (1 Macc. 2:44–48). Jesus' question to the armed band that arrested him exposed their estimate of him and of his following. "Have you come out as against a *lestev*, that is, 'revolutionary' or 'insurrectionist,' with swords and clubs to capture me?" (14:48). The RSV translation obscures the political overtones of the arrest. The arresting band's perception of Jesus matched the disciples'. It was Jesus' refusal to resist arrest with force and thus fulfill the political expectations of the disciples that broke their bond to him.

The disciples had followed Jesus in hopes of a holy war. As

they drew near to Jerusalem, they pledged their willingness to run the risks to their personal safety in the war. When Jesus refused to act in keeping with their political expectations, they withdrew their loyalty to him. From the point of view of their Davidic, Zealot politics, it was not that they had failed Jesus, but that he had failed them. In the bitterness of their disappointment with Jesus, Peter spoke the ironic truth when he swore to his accusers, "I do not know this man of whom you speak" (14:71). The man whom he had known was pretender to the Davidic throne. He did not know this weakling who gave in just when it was time to fight.

By exposing the misunderstanding of the first disciples during the earthly career of Jesus, Mark warned disciples in his time against making the same mistake with respect to Jesus' second, heavenly coming. Mark's argument was that, just as discipleship based on Davidic politics was mistaken in Jesus' day, so also disciples in Mark's time must not make the same mistake by interpreting the war as the vehicle of Jesus' return. Mark argued that divine necessity and the mandate of Scripture required that Jesus come the second time on clouds of glory as the revealed Son of man. The second coming as the revealed cosmic Son of man would be in accord with the first coming of the hidden, parabolic Son of man.

Directions for Witnessing

Mark used the passion of Jesus not only to correct the cardinal error in discipleship, but also to display and support the positive aspects of discipleship. As we have seen, Mark's community looked to Jesus of the tradition as the hidden form of the risen Son of man showing them how to follow him in their time. Almost every element in Mark's description of his own community under persecution had its counterpart in the career of Jesus. If, as I believe, the passion narrative was planned by Mark to follow the three predictions of the passion which he composed, then it is natural to expect that chapter thirteen also had a part in structuring that narrative.

Verses 9 and 11 of chapter 13 speak of Mark's community

being "delivered up." The same verb appears in the second and third predictions. After the hearing before official Judaism, they "delivered" him to Pilate (15:1, 10). Finally, Pilate "delivered" him to be crucified (15:15). It is the same word used for betrayal by Judas (14:10, 11, 18, 21, 41, 42, 44). Verse 12 has family members delivering up (in the sense of betrayal) one another to death as Judas betrayed Jesus.

Marcan Christians were being handed over to local "sanhedrin" of synagogues (13:9) just as Jesus was handed over to the Great Sanhedrin (14:55; 15:1).

Marcan disciples were being beaten (13:9) just as Jesus had been scourged (15:15).

Marcan Christians were arraigned before governors and kings (13:9) just as Jesus had been brought before Pilate (15:1ff).

However inevitable suffering under persecution may have been, it was not an end in itself. It served the mission of the movement by becoming an occasion for witness—"you will stand before governors and kings for my sake to bear testimony before them" (13:). The positive meaning of the era of tribulation preceding the End was that it provided opportunity to preach the gospel to all nations (13:10). This gentile mission shared the same divine necessity as the tribulation. "This (tribulation) must take place" (13:7) has its parallel in "And the gospel must first be preached to all nations..." (13:10). The tension in the time until the End came from the precarious balance between time enough to spread the gospel to the whole gentile world and not enough time for suffering to eliminate the elect and leave no one to witness! This was the terrible situation that Jesus faced in Gethsemane. He faced the fact in anticipation of the situation of Mark's community that though the cup of divine necessity could not guarantee his survival, it could become an occasion for witness—and even for Jesus a part of the gentile mission. The positive reaction of the centurion in charge of the crucifixion, "Truly this man was a son of God!" was comfort and pledge that Mark's church could be equally effective with their captors.

In the context of the missionary meaning of suffering, everything came to depend on having the right thing to say in the moment of trial. It is a tribute to the spirit of Marcan discipleship that the community had so internalized and appropriated Jesus' experience in Gethsemane that their only remaining anxiety in face of death was that they would have the right word of witness. "And when they deliver you up, do not be anxious beforehand what you are to say" (13:11). To meet this supreme crisis of discipleship, Mark's co-disciples experienced a special gift of the Spirit—the gift of appropriate witness in the hour of trial. "And when they bring you to trial and deliver you up, do not be anxious beforehand what you are to say, but say whatever is given you in that hour for it is not you who speak, but the Holy Spirit" (13:11). This is a highly significant experience for Marcan discipleship—probably their peak experience. This singleminded devotion to mission, in studied indifference to survival, is the epitome of denying self and taking up one's cross to follow Jesus that defines mature discipleship (8:34–37). This specific experience was meant to fulfill the prophecy of John the Baptist—"I have baptized you with water; but he will baptize you with the Holy Spirit" (1:8); we recall that the reply to James and John used the term "baptize" along with "cup" to symbolize the cost of discipleship.

The trauma Jesus faced in Gethsemane, wrestling with the divine necessity of the "cup," was the model for the trauma which Marcan Christians also suffered in arriving at the experience of the gift of appropriate witness in the hour of trial. The final admonition of chapter thirteen is a direct play on the experience of Gethsemane under the guise of waiting for the End. Verses 35–37 speak of "watching," "falling asleep" and the time of day (according to the Roman watches) all of which occur in the Gethsemane experience (14:17, 34, 37, 38). The "hour" of Jesus' arrest and trial (14:41) is parallel to the "hour" of Marcan witness (13:11).

It would be a mistake to imagine the gift of apt witness in the same class with speaking in tongues as though not being anxious beforehand were the same as not taking thought beforehand. The whole creative act of composing the book of Mark and especially the composition of the passion narrative were thoughtful preparation within the community of discipleship for "the hour" of witness. It is the essence of Marcan prophetic consciousness to take thoughtful account of both Old Testament tradition and of the tradition about Jesus as it was given them to do by the Holy Spirit. For in the prophetic movement within first century Judaism in the early church as well as in Qumran, the prophetic function turned on the charismatic, that is, gifted, application of tradition to the situation of the prophet and his or her community. The composition of chapter 13, the themes of divine necessity and scriptural fulfillment, and especially the prophetic self-consciousness of Mark all point to this gifted reflection as the basis of the witness of the Marcan community. Accordingly, the editor sets himself over against those prophets within the early church who did not take adequate or gifted account of tradition. No doubt one of the major aims behind the creation of the written gospel form was to correct the mistaken witness of false prophets within the early church. As we saw, the conditions attached to sending out the Twelve may well have been meant as restrictive checks on a thoughtless charismatic prophet movement within the church. But even those restrictions were inadequate without an authoritative statement of the normative meaning of the tradition. The composition of Mark and concomitant creation of the gospel form should be viewed as a prefiguring of the move to establish a New Testament canon. In the late second century, the church moved to counter the charismatic errors of Montanist prophets. Mark moved to counter the charismatic errors of Zealot prophets just as we must make a comparable move in our time to counter chauvinist, culture-bound Protestantism.

Mark meant the witness of Jesus in his hour of trial to set the pattern for disciples in Mark's day. Indeed, Jesus' responses to the high priest and to Pilate make as much or more sense for Mark's political situation as they do for Jesus'. The trials of Jesus follow the double pattern set in chapter thirteen of first the Jewish council, then the non-Jewish governor or king (13:9).

The issue which Jesus' Jewish accusers raised was the rumor that Jesus had said he would destroy the temple and build another heavenly one in three days (14:58). This accusation required no response at all since it failed to meet the test of support by two witnesses. The point here for Mark's day is that disciples should not support any role at all for the temple in the age to come.

False witnesses bore a variety of charges against Jesus but he refused to respond to any of them (14:61). Marcan Christians, likewise, were not to be distracted from the appropriate subject of their witness by the "red herrings" of false accusers.

The only issue before the council that Jesus was willing to address was the question of his messianic identity. The implication was that Mark's people should do the same. And in addressing that question, they should respond exactly as Jesus had. First, Jesus confessed that he was the Messiah. But in the same breath, he defined that Messiahship in terms of a heavenly Son of man, thus countering the mistaken identification of Messiah with the Davidic model. Mark's people were to do the same, that is, they were to assert that Jesus was indeed the Messiah but that his return would be an apocalyptic event in no way related to the Davidic pseudo-messiahs who claimed to be coming with the war against Rome.

It has always been difficult to see what the high priest and council found so immediately and obviously offensive in Jesus' admission to be the Messiah. The claim to messiahship was not heretical in first century Judaism. But the high priest called it "blasphemy" and thereby worthy of the death penalty. This makes less historical sense in the setting of 33 A.D. than if we shift the setting to the time of Mark during the war against Rome. Then it begins to make better sense as does the accusation with respect to the temple. The two issues at the trial of Jesus, the fate of the temple and the identity of the Messiah, were the crucial issues in the time of

Mark's community. When Marcan disciples refused to participate in or support the war, they would have been queried about the implications for the temple, that is, if the war were lost, the temple would go. Didn't they care? Their answer provided in chapter thirteen was that in their view of the divine plan, the temple was bound to be destroyed. The second question would have related to the war itself. "Do you not recognize that this is a holy war and that its leader is your Jesus returning in messianic glory?" To this, Mark's community replied, "This is not a holy war for us and Jesus will come again as the Son of man from heaven and not in the form of a Zealot leader." *This* would have been blasphemy! To speak against God's war and against Israel's leaders in it would have seemed blasphemous.

Exodus 22:28 links blasphemy against God and "speaking ill of a ruler of your people." When in chapter thirteen Mark's people called the leaders of the war pseudochrists and pseudoprophets (13:22), they would have been reviling God so far as the Zealots were concerned. Most probably, the indictment used against war resisters was blasphemy. What we see then in the interchange between Jesus and the Great Council was a model for the witness of Marcan Christians in their trials before Jewish councils during the war. The particular words of witness were to be left to the gift of the Spirit in that hour, but the substance of the testimony had been made clear. Before Jews, faithful Marcan martyrs were to make the point that Jesus was Messiah but a Son of man Messiah who was to come after the pattern of the vision in Daniel. The Zealot Messiah with the holy war as his vehicle was not God's way of bringing the End. If this mistaken war led to the destruction of the temple, so be it. It was necessary for these things to take place, but the End was not yet (13:7).

The pattern of Jesus' testimony suggested that the Marcan position with respect to the temple was not to be an explicit feature of their witness to Jews. When confronted with the testimony about the temple's destruction, Jesus chose not to respond. "But he was silent and made no answer" (14:61) so as not to distract from the positive point of witness. The fate of the temple was a matter for community understanding, not public discourse; the temple's destruction belonged to the tragedy of history, not to the Good News. (Here it is important to note that the Marcan witness did not dwell on the destruction as judgment.) Jesus had spoken up when his identity was at stake—that was the heart of the Good News—and following his example so should Marcan Christians.

Before Roman tribunals, the thrust of witness was to be somewhat different. The pattern for this witness was set by Jesus' conduct before Pilate. Before establishing the content of witness to the Romans, it is just as important to catch the mood of that witness. It was the same mood as in the encounter with Jews: poised control. Jesus made no defense of himself. For him, his fate was a foregone conclusion. Anything he had to say was not intended to influence the verdict one way or another. His survival was beside the point. That was a matter between him and God, not between him and his accusers, Jewish or Roman. This poise came from the fundamental conviction shared by Jesus and the Marcan community that in the hour of their trial and witness, events were in the hands of God and not in the hands of the accusers as the chief priest and Pilate supposed. "Have you no answer to make? See how many charges they bring against you" (15:4). The lessons of divine necessity and fulfillment of Scripture found in chapter thirteen and internalized at Gethsemane had prepared Jesus and Mark's community. This mood of poised control is underlined by the silence of Jesus before the badgering questions of both the chief priest (14:60) and Pilate (15:4, 5). At the root of this poise was the sure conviction that God was in control, not the Jews or the Romans.

The content of Jesus' witness before Pilate was less explicit than before the Sanhedrin. For Pilate, Jesus' identity was strictly a matter of Zealot politics. "Are you the King of the Jews?" meant, "Are you the revolutionary pretender to sovereignty over Palestine in place of Caesar and of me, Caesar's representative?" This title was not Pilate's idea but the charge which fellow Jews had brought to Pilate against Jesus (15:4a). Translated to Mark's setting, this would have meant that wherever Marcan Christians fell into the hands of Romans who had come to quell the rebellion, fellow Jews accused them to Rome of being revolutionaries.

Why did fellow Jews thus misrepresent Marcan Christians? Mark said out of envy or jealousy (15:10). Official Judaism had been jealous of Jesus' popularity with the common people. In territory reclaimed by the Roman legions as they moved into Palestine to put down the rebellion, Marcan Christians would have earned considerable credibility with the common people for their stand against the war which was now proving, as they had claimed, not to have been God's will. That would have caused Zealot envy. On top of that, the Marcan stance toward the law would have eased the relationship of Jews with Romans as Jews began to reconstruct the ties broken by the war. Marcan Christians were in effect offering a non-Pharisaic form of Judaism as the new Judaism to replace the parties that would collapse after the war. Pharisaic Jews, who were already planning their takeover as normative Judaism, would have been alert to this dangerous competition more acceptable to the nonobservant and lax common people. It would then have been to Pharisaic Judaism's obvious advantage to destroy the competition by representing them to Rome as an especially persistent form of Zealotism.

For Marcan Christians, this would have been an indictment almost impossible to refute to Romans who could not be expected to understand the Jewish distinction between a Davidic Messiah and a Danielic Messiah, between the kingdom of David and the kingdom of God. Any followers of a competitor to Caesar and the Empire, especially one whose takeover was imminent, would certainly be understood as seditious. What form should witness take in such an impossible situation?

When Pilate put the indictment which accusing fellow Jews had provided, namely, that he was King of the Jews, Jesus said in effect, "You say so; I do not" (15:2). That this was no answer to the question, verse four makes clear. "And Pilate asked him again, 'Have you no answer to make?'" Jesus simply refused to reply to this question. Jesus' refusal to discuss the christological question with Pilate did have its effect, "so that Pilate wondered" (15:5). Mark was saying to his contemporaries that when it comes to your witness before Roman courts, your manner may be more important than your message. In the final analysis, among Romans, the way Jesus had conducted himself was what had the most positive effect as witness. Not only Pilate, but the Roman centurion in charge of the crucifixion, had been deeply touched by Jesus' manner. When the centurion saw *how* he died, that elicited a deeply religious response. "Truly, this man was a Son of God" (15:39). It was by no means a Christian confession, but it did signal a shift from what had been until then merely a political proceeding to a religious experience. And this had been accomplished by the manner in which Jesus had accepted his humiliation, suffering, and death. Herein lay the lesson for the Marcan community.

Still, there was a hint in all this of the way the Marcan community could discuss christology with Romans once the political crisis had passed. Romans could be expected to make sense of Jesus as Son of God. The places in the book which hinted at this portrayal anticipated that Jesus, presented as Son of God, would become the basis for future witness to gentiles. In Jesus' trial, Mark was suggesting to his contemporaries that they put their witness to Jews in terms of a Son-of-man Messiah and to gentiles in terms of a Son-of-God Messiah.

Although Jesus refused to witness to his messiahship to Pilate, the events Mark portrayed constituted a defense against the indictment of Jesus as a Zealot King of the Jews. The people who accused Jesus of being a Zealot pled for the release of a true Zealot, Barabbas who had committed murder as part of an insurrection. This vignette had the effect of turning the tables on Jesus' accusers. They had accused Jesus of being a Zealot, but their own actions proved that they sided with Zealots. Mark was advising his contemporaries to let the war record of their accusers speak for itself. If they were falsely accusing Marcan Christians of being Zealots to the Romans while their own conduct made that very same case against them, Mark was advising his community to find a way to let the war record of their accusers convict them.

This, then, was the sum of the lesson of Jesus' conduct when summoned before Roman judges. Refuse to discuss Jesus' identity in terms of Zealot accusations. Let your manner itself be a witness. Hope for some recognition of the presence of God in that manner. Speak of Jesus as Son of God to your Roman jailers if they recognize that presence. Find a way to let the war record of your accusers count against them so as to expose jealousy as the true ground of their accusations. After all, you, not they, were right about the war.

To me, a Marcan setting for the passion narrative makes much better sense of the conduct of Jesus' trial before Jews and Romans than any attempt to explain it in terms of the conditions that prevailed in Jesus' day. The trial of Marcan disciples by Zealot Jews in the heat of the war would account for the summary and irregular proceedings against Jesus by the Sanhedrin. The same setting would account for execution without adequate grounds by Romans who were very sensitive to any hint of Zealot sympathy among Jews in the aftermath of revolt. The historical Pilate was not the kind of person who was so anxious to please a Jewish crowd that he would have released a convicted Zealot and condemned a rabbi against whom he knew, according to Mark's account, there was no true indictment. It makes better sense to suppose that the passion narrative is a riddle form of the persecution Marcan disciples suffered in the course of the Jewish war of 66–70 A.D. If Christians and Jews of today wish to use that narrative to discuss their relations, let them both realize that it has only an oblique relation to the actual death of Jesus. But for Christians who wish to be instructed in their obligation to witness, it has a direct and massive relevance— which is what we should have expected all along. "For whatever was written in former days was written for our instruction" rather than to satisfy historical curiosity.

Discipleship and American Politics

Now that we have seen the integral, intimate connection in Mark between discipleship and politics, there can be no continuing biblical warrant for private-party evangelism which seeks to avoid addressing political issues. When Billy Graham sought to avoid critical comment on the Vietnam War by saying he was a New Testament evangelist, not an Old Testament prophet, he showed that he had missed the point of what Mark, the New Testament evangelist, was doing. Mark's critical stance toward his nation's war came precisely from his gospel. The war provided the occasion to shape and focus that gospel. Indeed, the beginning of wisdom in the politics of the Son of man is to deny that any political arrangement including the American one can bring in the kingdom of God.

Repentance of worldly politics applies as much to public party romanticism as it does to private-party avoidance, although the forms of their politics are different. Private-party politics seeks to make the market the arbiter of public good. At its best, it claims that unequally gifted people ought to have equal access to the pursuit of happiness. But the market will distribute the rewards so that the goods received will be vastly different. That distribution is supposed to be just, but it disregards the massive fact that the socioeconomic system determines beforehand the advantages and disadvantages each person brings to the supposedly equal opportunity. In public-party politics, people deserve equal, minimal well-being in the form of food, housing, education, full employment, medical care, retirement income, regardless of the market's allocation of these goods. Government must correct the marketplace's distribution of well-being so as to redistribute the goods on the basis of an ideal of justice that prescribes a minimum humane standard of living. These are very different forms of politics. They are so different that their respective advocates are in continual, furious conflict. But party conflict masks the fact that both politics reflect a false presence of the kingdom. Both private- and public-party politics share the peculiarly American pretension that each of their politics are equivalents of the kingdom of God. Perhaps with the exceptions of Abraham Lincoln and Reinhold Niebuhr, all the chief spokespersons of the American dream, including its religious versions, have been hopelessly chauvinist—from Jonathan Edwards to John F. Kennedy, from Ben Franklin to Archie Bunker. All have supposed that there is some equivalent of divine destiny that leads inevitably to the kingdom of God as a version of the American arrangement.

Both public- and private-party versions of the American dream fail because they center their arrangement around something other than a symbolic equivalent of the Son of man. The private party pays lip service to the centrality of the Son of man but refuses to allow him to interfere with the lordship of the market. Indeed, the ultimate test of fellowship in that party is not religious commitment but economic ideology. The public party professes to center its program around the just God of the prophets, but the final criterion of action is the liberal ideal of human dignity. Anyone who shares this human ideal is a fellow instrument of the divine plan regardless of specific religious commitments or their complete absence. Jesus and the prophets put love of God above every other commitment because God is the ground of every just value. But the public party makes the love of God in personal terms an optional extra. At the heart of the failure of the public party to translate the vision of the classic prophets into modern terms is their neglect of the crucial fact that the community which the prophets addressed was a confessional community with a common devotion to Jahweh.

The public party tends to substitute devotion to the liberal democratic ideal for devotion to the one true God. These are not equivalent devotions. The touchstone of fellowship for the public party is a liberal ideology. This creates a political-cultural coalition as a substitute for the church. In spite of Reinhold Niebuhr's acute analysis of the cultural captivity of the public party, he never quite extricated himself from the hope, first, that a third party, and, then, that the Americans For Democratic Action (ADA), might become the substitute church. Mark's vision of the coming of the Son of man on clouds of glory hangs in judgment over both versions of the Protestant dream, condemning them as surely as it did the Zealot dream of his day. And it declares that though we have been claiming to be prophets by the authority of these dreams, we who serve them are pseudoprophets, and the Messiahs they enthrone, pseudochrists.

The Protestant parties have made America such an exception to the rule of history that they refuse to accept the lesson of the Marcan apocalyptic that no earthly political program, however much it may claim the sanction of Christian tradition, may be the cloud on which the Son of man comes. Given the American sense of manifest destiny, these dreams and their attendant turmoil "must take place, but the end is not yet." Public-party addiction to a utopian replay of the era of the classic Old Testament prophets, and the studied irrelevance of private-party attachment to a literal and imminent return, betray both into the posture of the disciples coming down from the mount of Transfiguration confused about what the rising from the dead of the Son of man might mean.

Typical American Protestant attempts to answer that question remind us (after many party announcements to the effect, "Look, here is the Christ," or "Look, there he is!") that the eschatological counterpart to belief in the resurrection of Jesus is the sure conviction that God's End to history must be a transhistorical event. This is the primary meaning of the parabolic presentation of the coming of the Son of man on clouds of heaven.

Perhaps a prerequisite of apocalyptic conviction is such thorough disappointment with merely historical hopes that they are finally abandoned. It was this disappointment in Israel that led eventually to the flowering of the apocalyptic vision. One of the striking and central characteristics of American culture in general and American Protestantism in particular has been its ebullient, irrepressible optimism. We have claimed that every human problem is soluable by Yankee industry and ingenuity. Justification by technology— better living through chemistry, computer programs, nuclear energy, etc.—this has been the peculiarly American version of justification by works. But there are signs now that history has become a serious problem even for Americans. No one can give assurance that nuclear weapons will not eventually lead to holocaust. In the attempt to harness nuclear energy for peaceful means, no one is able to ensure adequately for risk of accident. The problem of the safe disposal of nuclear waste is especially vexing and may contain the parable of our time. Nuclear technology unlocked the door that leads to the heart of the universe and in so doing, it promised to show the way to the eternal blessedness of cheap and everlasting energy. But the incidental price of that bonanza has turned out to be lethal wastes that promise to be just as eternal in their poisonous effects. The conventional wisdom, "There is no free lunch," has suddenly taken a macabre turn. Is it the story of the Tower of Babel in modern guise?

There are signs that Americans may at long last be ready to heed the lesson of apocalyptic. The politics of each party have had their day and ceased to be. Careful scrutiny of Kennedy's "Camelot" showed it as reluctant to take a timely stand for human rights at home as its conservative opposites; abroad, its "best and brightest" responded to the communist challenge with the same macho and paranoia as the least stylish cold warrior of the fifties. And when impious youth and blacks had the effrontery to criticize redemption in the form of the Great Society, its leader just withdrew in a peevish funk to the banks of the Pedernales to nurse his wounded messianic consciousness. Then the competition had its chance, led by one who could really face up to the communist threat abroad *and* who understood the realities of the world of business at home. What was more, this tough-minded realism was decked out with the religious trappings of White House Sunday worship by invitation, prayer breakfasts, and the pastoral care of the private party's chief of chaplains. "If God be for us, who can be against us?" The results were such conduct of foreign affairs as to completely demoralize the generation assigned to fight its war and the business community exposed *flagrante delicto* with the Committee to Reelect the President. Respect for business leadership fell to an all-time post-Depression low. Political and corporate institutions must struggle to recover public respect. And so far as the relationship of their piety and politics was concerned, the joke that circulated among businessmen about Richard Nixon attempting to fill an eighteen-minute gap with a Billy Graham sermon was cruelly to the point.

Perhaps it was partly Jerry Brown's theological training that led him to draw the moral from all of this, namely, that it is time for Americans to expect less from politics. Our common American heritage, reinforced by each party version, has been to expect redemption through our politics. The politics of the Son of man declares that redemption through politics was never possible, since politics is bound to history. Redemption leads beyond history. American Protestants ought finally to be ready for this message.

The Positive Lesson of an Apocalyptic Perspective

We need, however, to avoid making the negative lesson of apocalyptic the main one, although it may be the only lesson available to an unbelieving world. "Apocalyptic" connotes disaster in conventional discourse, for example, "acts of God" are catastrophes outside the bounds of reasonable assurance. In this context one often hears nuclear warfare equated with the biblical story of the End. The apocalyptic version of the End found in the New Testament does anticipate disaster. But this is not the part in the End drama that God provides; it is the part that we humans supply as we perversely pursue our variations on the politics of redemption. The truth is the exact reverse of conventional wisdom: Our acts are the disastrous ones beyond ensurance; "acts of God" are the ones that redeem the disasters we arrange. It is in this hope of the ultimate saving act of God beyond history through Jesus Christ as Son of man, that all descendants of Marcan discipleship live.

But Mark's heirs have a problem he did not have. Mark lived in the full flower of the apocalyptic world view. In that world view, the Danielic advent of a Son of man from heaven was a comfortable, reasonable, believable event. In the world view of the scientific American in general, and the public-party Protestant in particular, one might comfortably expect from heaven a sky diver, a 747, a space capsule, and, at the extreme limits of credibility, a visitor from outer space. But Jesus!—never!

This is the same problem neo-orthodoxy had—especially in its Barthian World Council discussion—that of convincing American Protestants that there was any such thing as the kingdom of God as a gift from heaven. The public party, by and large, simply rejected the idea. It had a long-standing theological bias against apocalypticism and a companion bias in favor of what it called prophetic realism. I am convinced that the major block to positive affirmation of the return of the Son of man by Americans has been their ingrained equivalent of Zealotism, namely, their quaint persuasion that the kingdom of God can come via American culture and politics without any disrupting intervention by God. For the public party, social action has made the coming of the Son of man superfluous. But once that peculiarly American hammerlock on history has been broken, there is to my mind no insuperable obstacle to the idea *per se* of the coming of the Son of man.

Wrestling With the Symbols

Belief in the resurrection of Jesus paves the way in principle for the recovery of belief in the return of the Son of man. Since public-party disciples do affirm the resurrection, they could by the same token affirm the return. The return of the Son of man is nothing more than the resurrection of Jesus applied to history. Return is just as much off the map of

sophisticated scientific reality as the resurrection. It does
ease the problem of the return to recall that a careful reading
of the variety of resurrection witness in the New Testament
shows that we are not bound to any single, simple, culture-
bound reconstruction of the resurrection event.[10] We have
seen for example how Mark left the Easter event itself in
parabolic shadow. I suggest that we proceed in the same
fashion with the return of the Son of man.

We should allow even greater room for interpretation
between Mark's form of witness to the coming of the Son of
man and the event itself that we do in the case of the
resurrection. In resurrection witness, the church described
an event it had already experienced. The description of the
return of the Son of man uses imagery borrowed not from
past experience, but from reading Daniel's vision of the
future. The future is notoriously elusive—even to certified
prophets. If we follow the lead of the rest of Mark we may
take the description in chapter thirteen as a parable whose
final meaning waits to be revealed by the event itself. For any
historical being, such a transhistorical happening is bound to
float in the mists of mystery. May we not learn to be
comfortable with a God and a risen Jesus who cannot be
contained in the earthen vessels of historical and scientific
imagination, let alone everyday chatter? Can we not see that
acts of God of the order of resurrection and the return of the
Son of man are bound to burst the worn wineskins of our
semantic carriers? I take the failure of language and concep-
tion in these cases to be more a sign that we are approaching
the unfathomable mystery of God than that we are trailing
off into nonsense. The nearer to God, the greater the
mystery. World views with their languages and their con-
ceptual programs come and go. Perhaps our attempt to
conceive the coming of the Son of man is somewhat like
earlier attempts to calculate the chronology of the End.
Suppose it is the case with both—"no one knows, not even
the angels in heaven, nor the Son, but only the Father"
(13:32).

Still, though strictly speaking inconceivable in terms of a

modern secular world view, the coming of the Son of man to end the ambiguity of history makes sense to the logic of faith. It is the logical extension of the transformation process already begun in the community of disciples. It is the logical extension of the selection process already begun in the call to discipleship. It is the logical extension of the process of discipleship that having followed the Son of man into suffering, disciples should someday follow him into exaltation.

There is a danger to discipleship in the expectation of shared exaltation, the one guarded against in the stories of the conversation about who is greatest and in the request of James and John. The answer is that the exaltation experience at the return of the Son of man is absolutely nontransferable into history. Only the first coming applies to discipleship within history and that mandates service instead of superiority. There is, Mark says, *some* correlation between discipleship within history and status at the return, but it is the inverse of the order within history. "Many that are first shall be last and the last first." For American Protestants, the recovery of the modesty of discipleship is crucial to the recovery of authentic discipleship. This-worldly triumphalism in the name of other-worldly biblical eschatology has been the besetting sin of American Protestantism.

Does this mean that American Protestants should lose their characteristic drive and their ingenuity born of the conviction that every problem has a solution if we work hard enough and dream grandly enough? No and yes. No, in the sense that true discipleship releases as much creative energy as triumphalism. Yes, in the sense that American confidence in itself, or lack thereof, regularly leads to grossly aggressive behavior that solves nothing, but only ministers to our hubristic need to flaunt our power in vain attempts to prove to ourselves and to the world that we are Number One. Vietnam was the perfect example. I am much more comfortable with the American symbol of the self-made man than I am with "one nation under God." At least then we know whom to blame.

In the recovery of an authentic eschatology for American

Protestants, everything depends on who is coming. In triumphalism one projects one's dreams of power onto a satisfying Messiah figure. In discipleship, the Son of man is one who "came not to be served but to serve and to give his life as a ransom for many." Triumphalism is a desperate form of self-affirmation. Discipleship's true eschatology, the politics of the Son of man, quietly accepts one's identity as a gift to be received rather than a prize to be won. That allows all the energy we ordinarily squander on posturing to flow into creative service. Perhaps the final watershed between triumphalism and the politics of the Son of man is that with triumphalism you do not really need to believe in the Son of man; in discipleship you must. Discipleship cannot be faked. Without the compensation of intimacy with the Son of man there is too much to lose.

Before the time of the final advent, everything depends on clarifying the difference between triumphalism and the politics of the Son of man. Witnessing to the difference for the future and offering the intimacy of discipleship for now, this is what one does "until the Messiah comes." This is what we found Mark's people doing. This is what American Protestants need to be about beyond each party's version of triumphalism.

The triumphalism of the private party calls for return to *laissez-faire* capitalism and a strong America equated with the kingdom of God. The public party triumph would be to expand the social services of government into a progressive welfare state, that is, an updated version of the New Deal that would carry forward the gains in human rights begun in the sixties. At the moment, the major fronts would be the reenforcement of affirmative action in face of the backlash of reverse discrimination and the increased monitoring of the industrial enterprise to upgrade the environment at home and to serve the aspirations of developing countries abroad. Neither of these deserves the imprimature of the Son of man as equivalents of his reign.

In Mark's experience this clarifying witness met punishing resistance. Of course, it would be paranoid of American

Protestants to expect to be put to death by civil and religious courts for this witness. Confrontation between courts and disciples in America will mainly have to do with clarifying what love of one's neighbor means for discipleship. The witness unto death of many martyrs who have gone before has won us the privilege of witnessing with our lives rather than our deaths. We should not feel deprived. The root of the word "martyr" is "to witness" not "to die." It is the circumstances that determine the secondary connotation. American circumstances condemn us to live our martyrdom.

Still, there may be punishing consequences. To begin with, the main bar of witness for American Protestants will be mostly the altogether informal courts of peers within one's own party. One's fellow and sister party members will immediately conclude that having broken party ranks the accused must be going over to the other side. Then one will be treated as the opposition within the ongoing power struggle of divided Protestantism. In the sense that your former party members turn against you, there is a parallel to Mark's community experience. It was family who turned them in for punishment as traitors. That was the unkindest cut of all. It is when former friends and supporters turn against you that you feel "hated by all."

The lost of party support is no small loss in present-day Protestantism. Divided as it is there is little community outside the parties. In discipleship we are called to be with one another as well as with Jesus, which means to depend on one another. Party support becomes especially vital when party theologies tend to distort, disparage, or overlook the support that comes from being with Jesus. In this case the party, by default, becomes the main religious life-support system. One can only risk the break with primary party dependency when the sense of the presence of the risen, and coming, Son of man is so strong that it can bear one up until fresh communities of the Son of man form.

Hopeful Signs
Given the grace to make the break, I do not think one need wait too long for fresh community. The Chicago Declaration

of 1973 was a sign, as is the sudden escalation of subscriptions to *Sojourners* and *The Other Side*, that the winds of the Spirit are blowing to form new configurations of Protestants gathered around some variation on the politics of the Son of man. Most of the people who declare that they feel moved in this direction were formerly fundamentalist or charismatic private-party types. Their old party colleagues have lost no time in finding a way to declare them deviants. They have been dubbed "radical evangelicals." As anyone knows who is familiar with Protestant infighting, "radical" is a code word in the private party for everything they find most offensive in the public party. It connotes an enemy of traditional values, evangelical religion, and civil order. For them, it is not so much that radical evangelicals actually act these things out *yet*. It is just that they are bound to sooner or later. Here is one more weary indication that the parties have so atrophied Protestantism that it is impossible for each party to imagine an alternative to one's position other than the enemy's. So the unkind cuts will be made, but the fresh, invigorating piety of the Son of man will more than compensate for the temporary loss of psychic support from party regulars.

There will need to be a shakedown period before radical evangelicals develop a full-blown equivalent to what I have called a politics of the Son of man. Many radical evangelicals have just discovered anabaptist Protestants in the left-wing tradition of the Reformation. Some are at the moment entranced with their vision of the kingdom of God which is so bright and so right that it must be possible to implement in this world without compromise, particularly in America. This is the perennial American Protestant utopian tradition asserting itself once again. We may have a Christian America if true believers really press. That expectation of an effective earthly politics of the kingdom of God is what I catch from time to time in the pitch of editorial voice in the radical evangelical publications. It is as if to say, "the public party has had the right social goals in mind, but they were not converted enough or Bible-believing enough to bring it off. We are. And we will." The real problem is not that the public party does not believe hard enough or try hard enough. It is not that their devotion is not deep enough. The trouble is their eschatology is outrageous. The politics of the Son of man declares that realization of the kingdom of God in this world is just not possible.

Many of the radical evangelicals will come to realize this because of their commitment to the Bible. Their commitment to a biblical life-style is the most definitive mark of radical evangelicals alongside their advocacy of fundamental social change. A careful, critical reading of the New Testament can correct the misplaced expectations for redemptive change in the world. The New Testament does not teach us to expect it. Indeed, the apocalyptic element in all of its witness explains why it cannot be. People who use the New Testament to imply that through their efforts the world can be transformed into the kingdom of God misuse the New Testament.

This misuse of the New Testament usually takes one of two forms. It rearranges the eschatological drama so that transformation in the world occurs before and independent of the return of the Son of man. That has been the overwhelming position of American Protestantism since Jonathan Edwards. Robert Handy tells the story of this misapplication of eschatology in *Christian America*. Richard Niebuhr also chronicled this tradition in his *The Kingdom of God in America*. That book and all his theology left this social perfectionist strain in American Protestantism unchallenged and unresolved.[12] So it continues. This perfectionist expectation of redemptive change in the world overlooks a key event in the eschatological drama. At some point evil and its agents, angelic and human, are sorted out of the mix of history. The elect are gathered. Wheat and tares are separated. Only repentant, believing disciples remain. The problem of evil is resolved. Then, and only then, redemption gets full social expression—but that will be in the age to come. The fundamental insight of the apocalyptic vision is that the element of evil in the world absolutely forbids any complete realization of the kingdom of God here. Americans do not want to believe this. Biblical people must.

The second misuse of the New Testament witness is to

transfer the language of redemption, rebirth, and new creation from the realm of discipleship to the world at large.
Richard Niebuhr did this with John's language of rebirth
even though he recognized that John had not.[13] "Transformation" is the public party's code word for redemption
and rebirth applied to persons and institutions. It argues for
the possibility of this transformation, without faith in the
Son of man, on the basis of creation and common grace. The
New Testament nowhere supports such a distortion of its
offer and promise of redemption. The fundamental change
for which the politics of the Son of man calls can only be
forshadowed among devoted disciples of the Son of man. The
measure in which that becomes a force for reforming change
in the world depends on the quality and quantity of the
leavening lump of the people of God.

It follows that the most immediate, this-worldly relevance
of the politics of the Son of man bears more on discipleship
than on the world. In Mark's time it called for radical change
among the traditional people of God. Translated to our time
that means that the most radical change called for in this
world is in the churches. The churches provide true transformation a place in the world. Without such a place transformation must remain so utopian for the world as to be
beyond its ken. Curiously, I find little of this call to the
churches in the radical evangelical literature.

May it be the result of the private-party background of
most radical evangelicals?

The redemptive change, the transformation in the world
that the politics of discipleship calls for and expects is among
the people of God and not in society at large. This is the social
change in the world that is possible without falling into
utopian perfectionism. Because the world organizes itself in
disregard of God, there is no place (utopia) in it, as world,
from which to mount the social transformation that belongs
to the kingdom of God. The reforming effects which the
early church did experience in its world emerged from the
base of a transformed people of God. Herein lies the solution
to the mystery of how the early church had such a massive

effect on a world it did not even intend to change. The same was true of the relation of the colonial church and pre-revolutionary America. The crucial factor is the quality of life, personal and corporate, of the people of God. The reforming effect which the church may have in the world is directly proportional to the level of transformation within the people of God. That is the major lesson history teaches about social change and the churches.[14]

The public party misses this point because it jettisoned piety in its simpleminded devotion to social change. The private party's piety has not led to the social change inevitable in classic piety because it is a bogus piety designed to forestall just that kind of effect on the world, which is one of the marks of true piety. Blinded by party platform to the crucial factor in social change, the public party groped for a substitute and supposed to find it in the factor of power. What it forgot was that the fundamental basis of power in society lies in the fundamental convictions of that society. It is ironic that this factor should be overlooked since it is a keystone in the political theory of the public party—that the power to govern is grounded in the consent of the governed. By the same token, the quality of consensus in a society determines the way power will be exercised and toward what ends. Without genuine connection to consensus, social power is Machiavellian, manipulative, and tyrannical. How incongrous! The public party tends to build a theory of social change on a covert base of tyrannical manipulation. Perhaps at some level the public party recognizes that without supporting piety, power in the form of manipulation is all that is left.

However that may be, my main point is that public-party policy for social change is one of the major American forms of cheap grace. It supposes to change the world regardless of the quality of life in the churches. It fools itself but not the world. The mystery of the politics of the Son of man is that it brought and can still bring greater and more fundamental change in a world it hardly intended to alter than all the intentional maneuvering of twentieth-century churches bent on changing the world.

A New Consciousness

At this point I may be easily misunderstood. I do not mean to depreciate the calls for justice put forth by the radical evangelicals. As we shall see in the next chapter, they represent the best possibility of recovering the adventure we prize. Nor do I wish to discourage the continuation of traditional public-party concerns and programs for justice. Until some new wave arrives in the churches they will continue to be our only claim to continuity with the great tradition of protest and reformation in the world which is one-half of Christian, let alone Protestant, identity. At this point I am pleading for a change of consciousness as fundamental to future programs of action. I am claiming that the hard realities of a continuing unjust world require a motivational base that is capable of working unceasingly for incremental changes in justice undaunted by the failure to resolve issues of deepest concern in a world that seems to care little for its own survival, let alone for justice. We need a consciousness among disciples that will stay poised and graceful under pressure; that although it may fail to achieve its goals, keeps setting fresh ones; that lives continually in the shadow of tragedy without losing heart; that continues the justice venture life-long without threat of burn-out. When the answer to burn-out, perhaps the most characteristic symptom of our time among servants of justice, is found in a fresh apocalyptic consciousness, Americans may enter into a new era of the struggle for justice in modern times.

This era will be grounded in a fresh realization of the presence among us of the risen Son of man still suffering with us the agonies of injustice now, and in the certain hope that issues of justice will be resolved at the point when he returns as Son of man triumphant. In terms of spiritual growth, this new consciousness would equal the dawning of a discipleship of maturity.

Lest the negative lesson of the politics of the Son of man leave us suspended above the earth on clouds of heavenly irrelevance, we need now to turn to what discipleship does to life in and for the world once American Protestants have given up their dreams.

•9•

Son-of-man Discipleship in Practice

The Question of Taxes to Caesar

Having freed us from our utopian dreams, Son-of-man politics leads us back to Son-of-man discipleship. The vision of the Son of man at the End frees us to pick up the thread of following the resurrected Son of man down the roads of our own Galilees. The fact that the politics of the Son of man jettisons the pseudoredemptive politics of the American Protestant tradition does not mean that the disciple has no political obligations in the world. Indeed, the refusal of Marcan Christians to help in the revolt against Rome implied some sanction of the Roman Empire and its arrangements with the Jewish people. We must not be blinded to this sanction by the heightened expectation of Mark's community that the Son of man would come very soon on clouds of glory to displace Roman order along with all the other orders of this present evil age. Until that bright event the commitment of Marcan disciples to the gentile mission meant that Roman order would continue to be the umbrella under which that mission would go forward. However temporary, Rome was very important to the mission. This meant that Marcan disciples had to work out some posture toward Rome until the end came. The story of the question to Jesus about paying taxes to Caesar illustrates the position which the Marcan community took. The question the Pharisees and some Herodians put was exactly the one Mark needed to answer: "Is it lawful to pay taxes to Caesar, or not?" (12:14) that is, is it in keeping with the will of God to acknowledge the legitimacy of the Roman order by submitting to its taxation?

The importance of this story for Mark is suggested by its appearance in a series of four controversies with Judaism that climax the public ministry of Jesus. Before Jesus finished teaching, Mark had him address the four most vexing issues between Mark and the Jewish community that was rejecting and persecuting his church. As we have seen, the surface issue was the war. The question about taxes addressed that issue at a more fundamental level. Since 6 A.D., Rome had collected a tax on every Jewish adult. Zealots refused to pay, making it a test of national loyalty. The hope of the questioners had been to trap Jesus into classifying himself with the Zealots just as Mark's community was being pressed by Zealots to side with the war.

The core verse of the story is no doubt an authentic saying of Jesus, "Render to Caesar the things that are Caesar's, and to God the things that are God's" (12:17). In Jesus' time it represented a skillful rejoinder in a typical rabbinic exchange, the point of which was not necessarily to address the substance of an issue, but to show which side had the sharpest wit in the verbal game of thrust and parry. At that level, Jesus won and the opponents "were amazed at him" (12:17). In this setting his reply merely followed the maxim that lost property should be returned to its owner with no questions asked.

For Mark and for us more is at stake. The story was preserved to guide the church in its relationship with orders of the unbelieving world rather than to display Jesus' skill at verbal fencing. For this purpose, the details of the story work beautifully. Jesus was asked for a denarius to be brought, a silver coin with Tiberius' bust on one side and his mother Livia represented on the other. The abbreviated sacred inscription read; "Tiberius Caesar, son of the divine Augustus, high priest." The issuance of coinage established the right of a ruler to the territory where the coins circulated and the money itself was understood to be the actual property of the sovereign. By getting the opponents to produce and handle a coin, Jesus, in effect, forced them to acknowledge Caesar's sovereignty even though it challenged Jewish monotheism. That accorded with the positions of the Herodians who saw no issue at all and of the Pharisees who claimed providential justification for the hegemony of Rome over Israel. It is this Pharisaic position which Paul reflected in his famous advice in Romans 13:1–7. "Let every person be subject to the governing authorities. For there is no authority except from God, and those that exist have been instituted by God " (13:1).

Paul could adopt this relatively sanguine view of Roman order so long as it served the gentile mission by shielding him from Jewish persecution. Paul's own martyrdom at the hands of Rome and the persecution of Marcan Christians by Roman courts prompted the church to recover Jesus' teaching as more appropriate given the benefit of longer experience with Rome. The second half of Jesus' dictum "and to God the things that are God's," avoided endorsing the Pharisaic position. By this he reserved to God a sphere within the world where Caesar's sovereignty did not apply.

The other position Jesus avoided was the Zealot one. "Render (give back) to Caesar the things that are Caesar's," accepted a tax on Jews which Zealots claimed only a revolutionary government had the right to levy.

The error of the Pharisaic position was to accept the Roman order as the final one in this world. The Zealot error was to suppose that only a Jewish state was the acceptable worldly order. Jesus' alternative to both of these errors was what we have been calling the politics of the Son of man. It was two-sided. *God's* order would only come at the end of the age—that is the meaning of "and to God the things that are God's." But until that time the disciple must come to terms with the interim order, granting to it some rights while rejecting its idolatrous claim to be the divine order. Jesus' position grounded the application of discipleship to the orders of this world.

The first lesson of Jesus' position for American Protestants is to resist the inevitable and perennial tendency of worldly orders to claim for themselves unreserved divine sanction. The major and eternal point of Jesus' answer is that Caesar's things and God's things are never the same. This applies not just to political arrangements but to all worldly arrangements, for they all intertwine. The symbol of the coin at the heart of the story displays the fundamental economic aspect of all political arrangements. To have Caesar's politics was also to have Caesar's economics. Therefore, by extension, Caesar's economics and God's economics are never the same any more than Caesar's politics and God's politics are ever the same.

Perhaps Jesus' point was easier to catch in his day when the coins displayed obviously pagan symbols. It would be confusion of the most subtly pernicious kind to mint money using both Caesar's image and God's image. The United States attempts just that when it issues money with George Washington on one side and "In God We Trust" on the other. It is elementary for disciples of Jesus that the God on the reverse side cannot be the God Christians confess. Likewise, the economic arrangements this strange god legitimates cannot be the economics of the reign of the God who is the Father of our Lord and Saviour, Jesus Christ. The god on this money is the patron of American pluralism referred to in Eisenhower's famous dictum noted before: "Our government," he said in 1954, and he might have said our economics as well, "makes no sense unless it is founded on a deeply felt religious faith—and I don't care what it is." The god Eisenhower refused to specify is the god of enlightenment deism. Its right hand is the invisible hand of Adam Smith. Christian monotheism knows better than to confuse its God with this pretender. Thus, the Christian with more than a grade-school equivalency in discipleship knows that he or she enters strange territory when trodding the ground at the feet of this bizarre patron of American pluralism.

Responsibility in the "World"

It was a comfort to Mark's people in face of the pretentious and idolatrous claims of Rome to know that the order that coin represented would last for a limited time only. Marcan disciples knew enough to trace Roman order not to God but to the true rulers of this age, Satan and the demons. The Marcan Christian was guided in the practice of discipleship by the sure conviction that the jury-rigged compromise with justice designed by a committee of demons, which we call the orders of the world, was a temporary arrangement. This estimate of the world was part and parcel of the apocalyptic viewpoint that we saw at the base of Mark's world view. The importance of these assumptions about the orders of the world shared by every New Testament witness cannot be overemphasized. The "world" is a temporary arrangement. The "world" is a fateful arrangement imposed by superhuman demonic powers. For in the apocalyptic vision, the world was seen as the arena of social and psychological forces that work with demon-like power and compulsion against humankind's well-being. It was the prophetic unmasking of these demonic forces as our own creations that set us on the road to responsible reaction against them. In this context the New Testament obligations to preach and heal take on broader ramifications.

Given these two assumptions, the disciples' complete responsibility toward the world was solely preaching and healing, if we include in healing all charitable relief of need. Healing miracles were but the most dramatic instance of a charity that relieved individual need whenever it appeared in personal contact with others. The whole duty of discipleship was witness and charity; that was it—while watching and waiting for the near end. By self-denying faithfulness to this double duty, the earliest church influenced the Western world massively.

But with the passage of time and the rise of a modern view of society, the charity mode of discipleship in the world changes and expands. The passage of time brings with it the realization that the orders of this world with their exploitative, inhumane, and oppressive effects deserve more attention since they have such continuing effect on the neighbors whom we love. To paraphrase the author of 1 John, "If anyone sees the continuing effect of systemic social evil on one's neighbor in need yet closes his heart against that insight, how does God's love abide in him?"

But even with this recognition, a fateful view of the structures of society long prevented the Christian from accepting responsibility to change the arrangements. Exorcism is the traditional symbol for escape from the clutches of fateful societal arrangements *while leaving those arrangements in place.* It was an enduring contribution of apocalyptic dualism to recognize the demonic quality of worldly orders. The drawback of apocalyptic dualism was that it understood those orders to be so entrenched that people were powerless to change them. There was nothing to do but wait for God to act at the End. However, with the rise of a less enchanted view of society, a fuller scope for discipleship came to light. When the arrangements of this world come to be seen as creations of human beings and not of supernatural powers, we begin to realize that, having created them, human beings have the capacity to change them. With the capacity to change the arrangements that deeply affect the neighbors we love comes the obligation in love to change them.

These two realizations, the continuing and human character of worldly order, never dawned on the church of the New Testament. Therefore, the New Testament contains no explicit charge to change social arrangements. With the dawning of these realizations the love of neighbor at the heart of discipleship mandates the expansion of that love to include social change. This mandate was at the heart of the Chicago Declaration. On Thanksgiving Day, 1973, a gathering of evangelicals expressed it this way: "We acknowledge that God requires love. But we have not demonstrated the love of God to those suffering social abuses."

At this point one's doctrine of the relation of the Word of God to the Bible can become crucial. If one holds to a doctrine of verbal inerrancy in the form that prohibits any divine directive to the Church that is not explicitly expressed in the New Testament, one can use that doctrine to shield oneself from fresh guidance of the Spirit.[1] But then the Bible is used as a letter that kills rather than as a vehicle of the Spirit that gives life. The greatest single defect in the theology of the private party since its inception has been the tendency to use a special doctrine of inspiration to fend off the divine mandate to love one's neighbor in the form of social change. It is just this view of Scripture used to this unscriptural end that drapes the private party with the mantle of legalism, if by legalism we mean the manipulation of tradition in order to avoid the full obligation to love one's neighbor which that tradition so obviously enjoins. It is high time for Protestants to protest this trammeling of the Word of God by their own tradition as much as they ever protested comparable abuses of the medieval church.

Discipleship as the Pursuit of Justice

What this boils down to is that with time and the realization that we create the structures of life, love of neighbor requires that we give at least as much attention to these structures as we do to charitable relief of their consequences. In other words, love sooner or later calls for justice. For this discussion let us agree to mean by justice the concern that social structures deliver well-being to my neighbor more fairly. Politics and economics are the primary orders so far as justice is concerned. In love expressed as justice, the disciple insists that the orders of society be administered and, where necessary, reformed so that the goods of the world be distributed more fairly to my neighbor. It is this love working itself out in justice that continues the spirit of New Testament discipleship while adjusting its form for the unexpected continuation of this world and the modern realization that we humans have the decisive hand in creating and managing its arrangements.

At the outset we sought some way of coming to terms with discipleship's obligation in the world once we have jettisoned the American expectation of its redemption. Jesus' saying, "Render unto Caesar the things that are Caesar's," has led us to see that in love, the ground of this autonomy for the orders of the world is justice. Perhaps it would be helpful to say that whereas American Protestants used to look at the orders of their world in terms of redemption, the politics of the Son of man leads us now instead to evaluate them in terms of ethics. To have made this distinction and then to stick with it frees discipleship for a fresh relationship with the world.

Justice means acting in keeping with what is morally upright or fair. Every society, institution, or organization has a working consensus about what is right and fair. It is often expressed formally in laws or regulations of some sort. Thus we speak, for example, of business ethics. This standard of what is right and fair in the world differs markedly from the standard of conduct called for in discipleship. It arises out of worldly considerations of what my neighbor deserves rather than from the love of neighbor taught and modeled in the career of Jesus. The worldly standard of justice usually falls short of what discipleship requires. Their two standards will almost always be different. As a consequence, a disciple is forced to practice a double standard, one appropriate for the world and the other for discipleship. American Protestants, accustomed to imposing their standard on society in their long-standing project to Christianize America, are often outraged at this idea when first broached. John Alexander, an editor of *The Other Side,* is a good example of this reaction. "We categorically reject a dual standard for personal and national morality... (Of course, the state *isn't* Christian, but sin is sin whether committed by Christians or non-Christians.) We get so upset we become incoherent when someone... suggests that morality and human rights are important but so are America's economic and military interests."[2]

The reason for the differing standards is the one Alexander alludes to but refuses to credit. Only disciples of Jesus acknowledge and accept his standard of love of neighbor. Indeed, insofar as disciples practice it, they do so only out of enabling intimacy with the risen Christ. It is not fair to impose this standard of conduct on those outside discipleship. As our lesson from the coin has shown, the things of Caesar and the things of God are not the same things—because they cannot be. People neither know nor are obligated to discipleship's standards by their citizenship in the world. Where discipleship standards are known, they cannot be lived out except in intimate following of the risen Christ. To lay the demands of discipleship on people unrelated to Christ not only asks the impossible, but is also unfair.

This is part of the meaning of the separation of church and state. Only Americans keep trespassing from both sides. Outsiders reach over to borrow churchly-sounding mottos like "In God We Trust" or "One Nation Under God" to sanctify their state while Protestants from their side launch crusades to Christianize the state. The result is resentment on both sides, the contamination of standards, and confusion of identity.

For discipleship, an accurate appreciation of the standard of justice in the world provides one of the major entrees to the world. Discipleship's love of neighbor begins expressing itself by insisting that one's neighbors be treated at least as fairly as justice requires, at work, at home, in the polling booth— wherever a consensus exists in the world about what is fair. This attention to what is often called "social ethics" is the beginning of discipleship in action. The world most often avoids responsibility for its own standards by simply ignoring them. Disciples provide a service to neighbors by taking the trouble to know those standards, calling attention to them, and seeing that the world's machinery of enforcement comes into play. Curiously, disciples devoted to grace begin to make their presence felt in the world as advocates of law. However incongruous it may seem, law is the manner in which the world makes way for love although law must always fall short of love's demands. Put another way, law is the form love takes when it is scaled down to the level of caring in the world.

It is crucial for disciples to recognize this fact. If they act in disregard of it, they are not perceived by the world as caring; just the opposite—the world perceives any attempt to impose more than justice as itself an unjust act. Such acts are taken not as evidence of caring but as evidence of tyrannical aggression. Nothing panics the world more than the specter of religious fanatics moving to impose their standards as simple justice when there is no consensus in the world that these standards are rooted in values the world can freely call its own. Prohibitionists were an example of this from the past; the Moral Majority is an example in the present. Needless to say, such agitation does not recommend religion to the world nor encourage the trust of prospective inquirers.

So the beginning of wisdom in the world is to differentiate the standards of discipleship from those of worldly justice. This does not mean that disciples accept the world's definition of justice as final. Discipling love will be able to see how worldly standards need to be raised to better serve neighbors. The world has ways to change its standards. Disciples will learn those ways and practice them, and thus make politics a service of persuasive love. By patiently advocating higher standards, seeing them through the process of public ratification, and following through by insisting on their fair administration, disciples enter the world on terms the world itself respects. The Quakers are preeminent in this discipleship of justice. None do this with greater consistency and devotion.

Discipleship as Response to Neighbors' Need

Commitment to justice of course does not eclipse what I have called charity. I am using charity in the sense of relief of one's neighbors' need. Charity continues to complete justice by seeking to relieve every human need worldly justice leaves unmet. All the New Testament injunctions and examples to go the second mile still apply. Indeed, that injunction is a perfect illustration. Roman law authorized the soldier to coerce foreign subjects to carry his kit one mile. That was justice. Christians volunteered to carry it an additional mile. That was charity. The world's justice gives up caring long before one's neighbors' needs are met. Love of neighbor keeps on caring after justice had done its bit and gone home. The world stops short of charity because to expend any more energy or goods on the neighbor would unfairly deprive the worldling of what the world declares he or she deserves. Disciple-love is willing voluntarily to forgo some of its just deserts to improve the lot of neighbors. It is this self-denying aspect of charity that is distinctive of discipleship. Jesus called attention to the woman who put only two mites into the temple treasury because it came out of her substance —in fact, it was her whole living. Those who gave much larger sums did not witness to discipling love because they "contributed out of their abundance" (Mk 12:44). It was this spirit of caring enough to dip into one's own living in order to share with a neighbor that drew the attention of the Western world to Christianity. The Roman emperor Julian took his fellow pagan to task by observing how disgraceful it was that Jews took care of their own "and the impious Galileans support not only their own poor but ours as well."[3]

Discipleship as Witness

Disciples need to consider how their love for neighbor connects with witness; otherwise, the two can pull in opposite directions. If the disciple proceeds through justice and charity to relieve the needs of neighbors only as the world defines their needs, he or she falls into a classic temptation. By using discipleship energy to satisfy worldly need alone, the disciple may convey the impression that there is no need for the peculiar benefit of discipleship—a graceful relationship with God through following Jesus. To stop at worldly need would endorse Satan's position that man lives by bread alone. Somehow disciples need in love to provide bread without stopping at bread. Love of neighbor expressed through justice and charity must sooner or later include witness to that same neighbor.

The division of Protestants into public and private parties destroys this essential wholeness. Public-party types distribute bread. Private-party types witness. American neighbors typically receive either one or the other. The result is that no one gets the true picture of Christianity. No wonder the decline of the effectiveness of the Protestant witness is traceable to this split. We need to rediscover the secret of the early church's effectiveness. In discussing the success of Christianity in outstripping rival religions, John Gager touches the essence of the matter: "It [Christianity] was neither totally religious, as were many pagan cults that met only for ritual activities, nor totally social, as were numerous voluntary associations. The key to its success lay precisely in the combination of the two."[4] Protestantism will succeed again among its rivals when it recombines justice and charity with witness.

The nature of discipleship compels the disciple to extend the invitation to discipleship by witnessing to neighbors in the world. The disciple experiences the intimacy, meaning, purpose, and community that comes in following the risen Christ as life's highest good. Not to want that experience for one's neighbor nor to take steps to share it would deny the meaning of love. So the activity of disciples in the world completes itself in fulfilling the mandate to become "fishers of men." Discipleship accomplishes its mission when it catches others up into that same discipleship.

One way the book of Mark suggests to couple witness to love occurs in connection with miracles. The strange exorcist, representing Mark's own church, cast out demons in Jesus' name (9:38, 39). That implies that Mark's church was accustomed to explain that the source of power and authority to perform works of love was the risen Christ whom they followed. They said in effect, "Don't thank us; thank the Son of man who sent us and who works through us." This use of Jesus' name with acts of love was common practice also among Mark's opponents (13:6) because it was common practice in the early church. It was not left to the recipients of acts of love to draw the conclusion that what was done for them stemmed from Jesus. The first century was full of miracle-workers acting in the power of many religious and philosophical "names." It was important to specify which name was involved. American Protestants who emphasize acts of justice and charity often impose upon themselves a sort of gag rule not to drag piety in lest they seem pretentious or over-righteous. The trouble with this reluctance is that it leads recipients to give credit to others that belongs to Christ. So works of love become occasions for witness by an accompanying word that specifies the name behind them. But the witness needs to go further in order to allow the experience of discipleship to reproduce itself in others.

Every disciple is responsible to perform the gospeling activity that was the early church's special way of sharing the experience of discipleship. As we saw, Mark created a new form for the gospel by taking what had been primarily sermon material and giving it narrative form instead. This is the responsibility of every disciple in the process of becoming a fisher of others. The disciple takes the sermons about Jesus shared with him in the preaching of the church, and through a response of repentance and faith turns them into stories of the specific ways the risen Jesus has touched his or her life. In this fashion each disciple adds experiences of Jesus from his or her life that continue the ongoing gospel story of following the risen Son of man. The ex-demoniac at Gerasim is a perfect model. Jesus instructed him, and all readers of Mark, "Go home to your friends, and tell them how much the Lord has done for you, and how he has had mercy on you" (5:19). In following this injunction the healed demoniac fulfilled the preaching function of discipleship as much as if he had been a prophet or apostle—that is, the first century's counterpart of today's clergy: "And he went away and began to proclaim [here is the early term for preaching] in the Decapolis how much Jesus had done for him; and all men marveled" (5:20).

This witnessing function of discipleship reinforces the American Protestant tradition of expecting a confession of faith at entrance into the church. Each of the two Great Awakenings reaffirmed this experiential component of the classic Protestant adventure. Sometime around the turn of the century, denominations substituted profession for confession. That meant that from then on all that prospective members had to do was *say* that they believed, with a formula such as "Jesus Christ is Lord and Saviour"; they no longer needed to relate how that had become a concrete experience in their lives. If Methodists are typical, no theological reason was given for the change. The old requirement just faded away—for the laity. The requirement of confession is still retained for candidates for the ministry as a remnant of the recognition that discipleship cannot complete itself in mission without a confessional experience to share. The tragedy is that now only clergy are expected to be equipped for witness. The next logical step followed when clergy alone were assigned the task of witnessing that belongs to all disciples. Most Protestants today have grown up in churches that have lost the expectation of witness as a routine function of all members. The recovery of authentic discipleship must remedy that. Every Protestant deserves some equivalent of the demoniac's experience, some healing experience of the touch of the risen Son of man.

In addition, each Protestant ought to be able to speak from an experience similar to the entrance of the four fishermen into discipleship—that is, the particular way in which Jesus' call interrupted his or her career and family commitments. Given Hoge's discovery of the typical Protestant caught up in the big three of family, career, and standard of living, we should expect the experience of the call of Christ to take control in just these areas of work and intimacy. It belongs to the content of witness not only to relate with joy the healing difference that the risen Christ has made in our lives, but also to tell just as concretely how his new control came to bear on job and home.

Work and family become the primary sphere in which discipleship is lived out. The Protestant will become aware of the standards of justice as they come to bear at work. Does the product meet just standards for quality? Does the process of production treat the environment of the work site fairly? How does that process affect the lives of the workers engaged in it? Does the worker receive a fair share of the income derived from marketing the goods and services? What is the standard for respect of the rights of employees by managers? These are questions of justice. By making such questions the main business at work rather than the worldly questions of what we must do to rise most quickly in status and salary, Protestants bring discipleship to bear on the marketplace. In so doing, we recover our true identity as Protestants and revive the adventure of taking piety out of the monastery into common life.

Questions of justice are as appropriate at home as at work. Loved ones are also capable of treating one another unfairly. Parents are not licensed, and there is very little supervision of the justice of their parenting. At the very least, parents ought to study carefully the developmental needs of their children at each stage of growth and take pains to provide the encouragement, support, and limit-setting that children need. It is not fair of parents to see their responsibility met by provision of the material needs and supplying anything else at their convenience.

I suspect love nowhere masks such a multitude of sins of unfairness as between spouses and lovers. We often suppose that intense affection automatically satisfies justice, but it just as often distracts attention from justice instead. As more spouses share the business of breadwinning, for example, it is only fair that bread-slicing as well be shared fairly. When both parents work, it becomes terribly important to see that children still get the parenting that in justice is their due.

At work and at home we come to take our companions for granted. But charity will always be alert to distress signals no matter how faint or close at hand. Our neighbor in need may turn out to be the spouse or co-worker who never seemed to need anything. It is the disciple's job, until the Son of man comes, to watch and not fall asleep. We saw how that means to avoid seduction by the world. It also means to watch continually for opportunities to express love to neighbors near and far through acts of justice and charity. Then justice and charity complete themselves, at work and at home, in specific witness to the supreme good of discipleship.

The Disciple as Martyr

Mark made it clear in chapter thirteen that some from his church were put to death because of their witness before Jewish and gentile courts. In this they followed Jesus by following his example. We have seen how Mark constructed the story of Jesus' suffering as a model for witnessing before the same kinds of courts. The plan of Mark's book suggests that Jesus completed his work in the world as witness by dying and that Mark's own people had done the same. The refusal of the first disciples to share this dying witness at the book's close suggests that the final lesson for the task of discipleship in the world has to do with the risks of witnessing. As we have seen, Jesus did not expect them to be able to die with him (14:28). But he foretold that James and John would eventually follow his example, as we know some of Mark's people did (10:39). But, we misinterpret Mark if we suppose he taught that death in the service of witnessing was a norm for discipleship. After all it was the members of Mark's church who, along with him, survived the persecution in Jerusalem that made the book and the continuing gentile mission possible. Not until the second century in the churches of Asia Minor did martyrdom come to be a technical term for witness sealed by death.[5] What the model of the suffering of Jesus together with the experience of Mark's church does teach is that the witness of discipleship always involves risk.

The risks of discipleship are especially important for Americans to consider. We saw that ever since the Gilded Age, from Russell Conwell to Billy Graham, the private party has promised wealth and success as rewards for discipleship. From Horace Bushnell to Harvey Cox, public-party people have looked for the kingdom of God around the next American corner. Protestants are typically at ease in their American world. The aura the churches project is one of comfort in the sure conviction that religion supports without question whatever projects Protestants happen to be pursuing. The result of such an ethos is that Protestantism witnesses more effectively to the American way of life than to the way of discipleship. More and more Americans of Protestant heritage are concluding that it saves time and resources to settle for the American way of life shorn of the inconveniences of institutional Protestantism. To turn this witness around so that it counts for discipleship instead of for the American way we must begin to communicate, however gently, that these two ways are not the same thing. What is more, they are likely to come into conflict. Finally, we shall have to say that to reach any kind of maturity in discipleship, one will have to risk forgoing some of the promised benefits of the American way. In short, Protestant disciples must expect in the course of their witness to become martyrs.

When I use "witness" and "martyr" together it is a play on words. "Witness" and "martyr" are at root the same word. I mean by "martyr" not one who dies in the process of witnessing but one whose witnessing costs something. This is its common meaning—one who sacrifices something of great value for the sake of principle.[6] But unless one achieves the notoriety of a Martin Luther King, Jr., few in our society are so threatened by the witness of faithful disciples that they feel compelled to kill them. In our times, in contrast to the classic periods of persecution, it will be the manner of our lives rather than the manner of our deaths that counts for witness.

Risk of a reduced standard of living is the natural implication of everything Mark has taught us about discipleship in the world. Anyone who goes to work with love and justice on his mind will sooner or later be detected as a nonconformist. The higher one rises on the organizational ladder, the greater the value placed on conformity. At higher levels, company decisions are supposed to reflect ever more clearly the operating values of the company unencumbered by competing values. If one cares for more than company values, production and profitability may suffer. In worldly terms, bleeding hearts may hemorrhage when the blood is their own but not when it is the company's.

Some of the resentment which devotees of justice inspire is understandable. People usually take unfair advantage of others because it is to their advantage and profit. They take advantage by exercising power over others. To redress unfair advantage means to threaten power and profit. In the competitive ideology underlying the American way, both power and profit are supreme goods. "How beautiful upon the mountains are the feet of him who brings good tidings" (Is 52:7). The feet of the bearers of the good news of justice will not seem beautiful upon the mountain to the unjust. This is exacerbated by the fact that society supports justice with police powers so that advocacy of justice always includes, however veiled, the threat of enforcement. That compounds the resentment.

It would be unfair to the American world to predict that it inevitably meets a concern for justice with resentment and penalty. There are corporations and other institutions in America that are led by strict policies of justice. But it is safe to say that as a general rule advocates of justice take a risk by their advocacy. It is precisely this willingness to take this risk that is a powerful component of discipleship witness. The risk of witness conveys as no mere words can that Christ controls the life of discipleship and that the benefits discipleship bestows far outweigh the rewards the world offers for conformity.

Transition to Mature Discipleship

The risk of discipleship was the underlying theme of Jesus' conversation with the disciples following the challenge to the rich man to give away his wealth. Peter, speaking for the disciples, wondered out loud what would become of *them*, seeing that *they* had left all to follow Jesus. The question grew out of the sudden awareness that the rewards of discipleship do not include riches in the ordinary sense. Jesus' answer assured the disciples, the Marcan church, and all the rest of us, that the rewards of discipleship are a hundred times more valuable than the losses it risks (Mk. 10:30). Even allowing for oriental exaggeration, that is impressive. The catch so far as the world is concerned—and for private-party theology— is that the hundredfold compensation is in the coin of discipleship, not in the coin of Caesar. Jesus said, "Truly, I say to you, there is no one who has left house or brothers or sisters or mother or father or children or lands for my sake and for the gospel, who will not receive a hundredfold now in this time, houses and brothers and sisters and mothers and children and lands, with persecutions, and in the age to come eternal life" (Mk. 10:29, 30). Most of the rewards of discipleship come in association with other disciples caught up in the common mission of love and witness.

Notice the difference between this promise of compensation for loss and the experience of Job who got all his restitution in worldly kind. The private party simply misrepresents discipleship when it confuses Jesus' teaching with the teaching of the Book of Job. The hundredfold income of discipleship cannot be calculated on the same basis as worldly income. Within discipleship worldly income may actually reach a plateau, if not decline.

The persecutions slipped in among the benefits points to the risk we are discussing. Nothing seals the truth of witness like risk. Moreover, risk becomes the occasion for others to ask why. That opens the door through which the invitation to discipleship extends itself. The mature disciple does not spend much time noting the risk of worldly loss. Inside discipleship, worldly loss for the sake of love and witness is not experienced as loss. It is quite the other way round. The loss would be in not continuing to follow Jesus into risky witness.

The stage of discipleship we are calling "risky witness" does not come without painful transition. It helps to know that what American Protestants go through to reach this stage is a common experience of discipleship in every time and place. Beyond the garden gate of eager commitment, there is a vale of tears laced with hesitation. The model itself was set in tears.

The experience of Jesus in Gethsemane is full of the marks of grieving—"greatly distressed and troubled," "very sorrowful, even to death" (14:33, 34). Something had to die. Jesus' prayer showed what it was. He had to die to the conviction that fulfilling his witness could not possibly cost him his life. "Abba Father, all things are possible to thee." Even at the crucifixion, Mark portrays him not yet reconciled to the loss that goes with witness. "My God, my God, why hast thou forsaken me?" (15:34). The transition to risky discipleship was only resolved in the resurrection.

We noted the parallels between the account of the garden and the record of Mark's own experience in chapter thirteen. The similarities show that Mark and his people went through the same kind of experience. By virtue of Jesus' model and his continuing support they weathered the same transition to risky witness. The sign that they had worked through the transition was their ability to stand before Jewish and Roman courts, concerned only to witness well, oblivious to the question of their own survival. To get to that point, we must suppose they went through the same dread, anger, grief, resentment, and panic Jesus modeled.

Our Personal Exorcism

So far American Protestants as a group have refused to make that transition. When the Gilded Age brought the prospect of worldly wealth for white, middle-class Protestants, most of our forebearers went the way of the rich man who opted not to follow Jesus "for he had great possessions" (Mark 10:22). As the church year makes its round we follow Jesus still through the events of Good Friday, but as observers, not participants. Our hearts are not in the pilgrimage, and so we are no more able to stay awake in the garden than were the original disciples. Prophets among us shout that there is a transition to make to a simpler way of living so that we may be unencumbered enough to take up the risky mission of discipleship. But for the most part we sleep on in the garden of the world's Gethsemanes.

The undercurrent of anguish, anger, and sadness in the calls of some prophetic Christians to awaken us from the spell of our indifference to the mission to which we have been called is understandable. What began as a nap in the Gethsemane of the Gilded Age has become something like a drug-induced coma in our time. But shouting will not help. We are possessed. There is no more prospect that we shall simplify our lives for prophets than that obese addicts of junk food will turn skinny for doctors. We do not need the threats of another John the Baptist. We need the power of Jesus, the exorcist. We have already named the personal demons of compulsive consumption tied to compulsive work in league with the interlocking triangle of family, career, and standard of living. The risen Son of man hovers over our unsatisfied lives offering to feed us the simple fare of his last supper— the bread and the cup of himself given to provide the nourishment for our true selfhood that we so desparately lack and yearn for. We have inherited our demons from our great-great-grandparents; our addiction is longstanding and deep.

The transition to other sources of satisfaction will surely bring the trauma of withdrawal, but the darkness of Good Friday will turn to the brightness of Easter for those who refuse to find their nourishment in the gospel of wealth. If those of us who are drawn to this transition find each other, it will not seem to last so long or to be so dark.

We have seen how the demons gather power from the social constructions of the reality around us. We need local congregations of Protestants who surround us with an atmosphere of worldly asceticism, that is, ascetic so far as the world's standard of consumption is concerned, but worldly insofar as we unburden ourselves so that we may be free to take on the burdens of charity and justice in the world.

It may encourage us to recall that the first disciples had inherited a similar addiction of even longer standing from their religious forebearers, and that Jesus was equal to it. The hope that can sustain us through the shift to reduced consumption is that Jesus still offers a hundredfold compensation in the company of other disciples with simple lifestyles, and most of all in a hundredfold intensity of intimacy with the Son of man. Everything about our history and the analysis of this book indicates that typical Protestants will begin to recover their adventure when they hear Jesus name their demon—compulsive, conspicuous, unnecessary consumption—including its whole support system at home and at work. The particular shape each of our exorcisms takes will provide for us the story with which we may begin to fulfill our commission to become fishers of others. Remember the former demoniac from the country of the Gerasenes who "began to proclaim in the Decapolis how much Jesus had done for him" (Mk. 5:20). Since the Gilded Age, the burden of the Protestant witness has been how much God has added to our possessions; now it is time to witness to how He relieves us from the burden of them.

No one faces risky discipleship without flinching. But the testimony of Peter and most of the other original companions of Jesus is that eventually it was more painful not to go on to this dangerous maturity than to hang back in safety. That, partly, is what Peter's tears meant at the crucifixion. He avoided taking the risk. But hanging back was painful too. Jesus was in custody, and Peter was safe. But instead of feeling relief, "he broke down and wept" (14:72). No one makes the transition to risky discipleship with civilized calm. In the throes of that transition we all feel tension, ambivalence, resentment of the God who puts us in such a situation. Resolution of the conflict within ourselves comes with the realization that it is we who have put ourselves in our uncomfortable situation by being so possessed by the world's version of good news.

It helps to apply to this transition a story Mark may have intended for that purpose. It is the story of the disciples sent to cross the sea alone while Jesus stayed behind in the hills to pray (6:42–52). They were told to make a passage—as we all are. The teaching about discipleship that dominates the last half of the Book of Mark is all about discipleship at risk. Mark matches teaching on discipleship with predictions of Jesus' suffering and death. The whole final lesson on discipleship takes place in the shadow of the cross. To be a disciple one must take up the cross, lose one's life, serve and not be served—perhaps give up one's life as a means of liberating many. The disciples catch the message and determine to carry on. When Jesus predicts their defection they all protest together, "If we must die with you, we will not deny you."

So the disciples rowed into the evening until they found themselves out on the sea without him. Then the wind rose against them so that they were distressed in rowing. It is a parable of Jesus' distress in Gethsemane. Jesus came walking —as related only in Mark's gospel—intending to pass them by. Jesus had the same passage to make they had, but he had resources to make the passage; they did not.

When they saw him they no more recognized him on the water than they recognized him at his arrest and crucifixion. In both cases he simply amazed them. Then he identified himself as the one equipped with the power of God to save them in their perilous passage. "Take heart, it is I; have no fear." Most important of all he got into the boat with them. We are not intended to make this passage alone though that is the way we set out. We only make this trip successfully when in mid-passage we discover a new intimacy with the risen Jesus. This new intimacy brings with it a new realization. The Jesus who just before had fed the multitude with loaves and fishes, can sustain us too in this crisis of discipleship. The disciples in the story were "utterly astounded for they did not understand about the loaves" (v.52). Thanks to

Mark we need not be so surprised. Jesus can help in startling ways as we pass through the supreme challenge of moving on toward mature discipleship.

Discipleship and the Churches

This brings us to the flotilla of Protestantism, that is, the institutional boats in which Protestantism makes its way. Where do the organized churches fit into risky discipleship? They fit as the gathering places of discipleship. All the lessons on discipleship say we are in this together—with Jesus, but also with one another. The final dimension of witnessing love is that discipleship cannot sustain itself and grow without discipling communities. So the work of discipleship in the world finally includes identifying others to share it with. One disadvantage of Mark's story is that it never talks explicitly about the church. But it is there all the same from the first calling of four. No one is pictured in solo discipleship. Howard Clark Kee speaks of the *community* of the new age. That community continues in the churches.

The churchly gatherings are the natural place for disciples to find each other to arrange for mutual support. They are the natural nests for fledgling disciples. New disciples need somewhere to go for the nourishment they so desperately require to mature and fly. The great failing of evangelism in the churches has been lack of a covenanted, committed band of disciples for fresh converts to join. One model was the class meeting of Methodism. Another was the Wednesday night prayer meeting of a generation ago. What is needed is a community of trust where the canons of discipleship are being openly and joyfully applied to every aspect of personal life. For such communities to flourish they most probably need the pastoral care and oversight of the resident clergy.

In Mark the gathered community was subservient to the movement of witnessing discipleship it embodied. It was the community of a movement. That movement continues in the Protestant churches of America. But the churches need awakening to that fact. They need to be reminded that they are first of all a movement and that as organizations their only reason for being is to be vehicles of that movement. In all candor, the churches are not awake to these facts of their lives. But we ought not to be surprised. The history of Protestantism in America is the story of awakening and dozing and awakening again.

In the absence of this awakened awareness, there is no guarantee that each parish includes discipleship gatherings or if it does, that they would be easy to identify or join. Where they exist they are likely to be enclaves of private-party piety with the strengths and weaknesses that implies. Such gatherings tend to be strong in their support of the conversion experience at the entrance to discipleship. They tend to be weak in nurturing the expansion of that witness into an appropriate discipling approach to the orders of society. But thank God they are there at all. Public-party types tend to gather apart from parish life with others who do not wish to be identified either with discipleship or the church. In such gatherings, social concern expands but anything distinctive of discipleship subsides in deference to politics.

So where they exist, discipling groups tend to be on the fringes of organized church life. No one is to blame. It is a familiar cultural story. In the Gilded Age our grand- and great-grandfathers ate sour grapes and we, their grand- and great-grandchildren's teeth have been set on edge. When for three generations and more the churches have been peopled with members who either misunderstood or avoided discipleship, it is not surprising that its present membership does not clamor for discipleship's special support systems. They do find plenty of other things to clamor for, so that clergy are not to blame, when they are at the mercy of the politics of voluntary organizations, where those who complain the most get the most attention from the leadership. Clergy are typically exhausted by congregational demands. There are no spare evenings or energy for creating discipling communities. Have the preoccupations of the organized churches locked out the peculiar needs of discipling communities?

I do not think so. More parishes include these communities than I have implied. But these exceptions aside, there is a special case to be made for them within the churches. If one searches the charters, disciplines, orders, and certainly the histories of Protestant churches, the needs of discipleship are constitutionally mandated. It is unjust of parishes not to provide them, whatever else they may program. Does that sound familiar? The law of the churches like the law of the world, requires something whether its citizens know or like it. Reform in the churches, like reform in the world can begin with justice. Only justice within the churches has a different standard than justice in the world. Worldly standards do not ask for discipleship support. The outrage is that this worldly indifference is imposed on the churches. I call this outrageous for that is what the world calls it when the churches seek to impose an unfair standard on the world. In the name of pluralism the world effectively blocks the church from programming for its most peculiar concerns. Reform needs to begin at home, and churchly constitutions provide the grounds for that reform.

To carry through that reform gracefully, the realities of organized church life need to be respected. When the pastor is invited to give a disproportionate share of his or her time to a relatively small proportion of a congregation, that can complicate parish life. It will take a concerted effort of the pastor and disciple-group members to avoid seeming elite and superior to others in the congregation. The congregation at large is likely to accept the discipling group only if it pitches into all the tasks the organization requires to maintain itself. We can take a lesson from Wesley's classes. They attended more, communed more, worked more, and gave more than their Anglican co-parishioners. It is especially important for disciples to earn and hold the respect of their fellow church members, for they constitute an obvious pond for discipleship fishing. As for the pastoral leaders, they can be expected to support disciples only so long as disciples themselves find ways to help make their professional role easier. At least they ought not to go out of their way to complicate it. As the churches arrange their priorities today, the pastor is already taking a risk to get involved with discipling.

With patience and grace, many congregations can be nurtured to the point that the onus would lie with those who prefer not to mature as disciples. When discipleship becomes policy in a congregation, that policy should be so interpreted and acted out that people who are shy of the commitments and risks feel fully welcome to share in the life of the congregation as far as they feel comfortable. Jesus was comfortable with a large crowd of uncommitted people while he ran a school for discipleship in their midst. The trick was not to let the crowd determine the curriculum, while welcoming them for matriculation whenever they became ready.

Signs of Hope

I have tried to show how Protestant America fell into a pattern similar to the tragic history of Israel. The way out was modeled in the New Testament by a community able to cope with tragedy in this world through an apocalyptic hope for resolution of that tragedy in a world to come. The apocalyptic consciousness that comes with this hope we have found modeled particularly in the community that produced Mark's gospel. Far from being a pathological response justifying withdrawal into sectarian survival until the End should come, that community showed us how that consciousness enables and empowers its devotees to engage fully in mission in a world that might otherwise have seemed overwhelming. If we avail ourselves of this apocalyptic consciousness adjusted for the social and psychological realities of our day, we may gain enough distance on our world to be able to return to embrace it in caring, ongoing mission, though we may never see encouraging effects from what we attempt. The Son of man who grounds this consciousness can by his encouraging presence enable us to suffer through lack of success while we continue for love's sake efforts we would otherwise have ceased long since. We are asking nothing less than that Christians begin to live by the New Testament faith they profess rather than continue to repeat in modern form the options that late Judaism had already worn out when the Marcan community emerged. In the process we shall not only recover our appropriate biblical roots but also recover the Protestant adventure with its double commitment to both personal and social liberation.

I have tried to make the case for this recovery on the twin basis of a cultural analysis of the history of American Protestantism and the description and application of an appropriate New Testament model. I trust this analysis stems from the same fresh winds that are already blowing in Protestant circles producing action and not merely reflection. All private-party evangelicals who have surmounted their aversion to issues of justice and are now enlarging their vision to include them are my spiritual brothers and sisters. I salute the movement among them that expressed itself in the Chicago Declaration at the Thanksgiving Workshop on Evangelicals and Social Concern in 1973 and that continues to express itself in *Sojourners* magazine. I am looking for a similar movement toward wholeness from leading public-party representatives. I salute the black church that never had reason to split into the parties I have described, having been excluded from a share in the life of the Gilded Age, and for Koinonia Farms and Clarence Jordan who shared that wholeness. I pray that the black churches in America will find as good reason to help their white brothers and sisters to recover wholeness as they have good reason to shun us. For I am persuaded that finally the recovery of the adventure to which we are being called must find working models in local congregations and not just in the lectures of academia or the editorial pages of magazines and journals. For showing one way that may happen, I salute the Church of the Saviour in Washington, D.C. and Gordon Cosby its pastor.

All these for me are signs of hope that what I have dreamed in this book is taking shape among the people of God in hundreds of places and ways whose story is not yet told because they are bent on fresh faithfulness, not publicity.

I have saved to the last one sign of hope that has had special significance for me—the United Farm Workers movement under the leadership of Cesar Chavez, a Catholic layman, assisted by a representative of the Protestant adventure, The Reverend Chris Hartmire. They together signify to me that once Protestants have recovered their classic adventure they will find themselves yoked with classically whole Christians from other traditions, and that from here on the promise for adventure in America will not be either Protestant or Catholic, but Christian.

Notes

Introduction, pp. 1–5

1. These are the labels suggested by Martin E. Marty, *Righteous Empire: The Protestant Experience in America* (New York: The Dial Press, Inc., 1970).
2. Kenneth A. Briggs, *The New York Times* (Sunday, Sept. 11, 1977): p. 7 of the "Week in Review."
3. Dean R. Hoge, *Division in the Protestant House* (Philadelphia: Westminster, 1976), p. 118. Chapter IV, "Church Commitment Today—How Strong?" summarizes the current research on the depth and character of Protestant commitment. I have found the book enormously helpful.
4. Hans von Campenhausen, *The Formation of the Christian Bible*, tr. by J.S. Baker (Philadelphia: Fortress Press, 1972), is the best explanation of how the various New Testament writings came to be included in the Bible.

PART I/*The Collapse of the Protestant Adventure*

Chapter 1   The European Prelude, pp. 9–15

1. Sidney E. Mead, "The 'Nation with the Soul of a Church,'" *Church History*, vol. 36, (1967), p. 275.
2. Max Weber, *The Protestant Ethic and the Spirit of Capitalism*, tr. by Talcott Parsons (Charles Scribner's Sons: New York, 1958), ch. IV, "The Religious Foundations of Worldly Asceticism," pp. 95–154.
3. It is important to note that Vatican II has ended the superior status of "the religious."

4. H. Richard Niebuhr, *The Kingdom of God in America* (New York: Harper & Row, 1937), p. 75.

5. Sidney E. Ahlstrom, *A Religious History of the American People* (New Haven: Yale University Press, 1972), p. 124. note 1.

6. For the history of the idea of "calling" see Karl Höll, "Die Geschichte des Wortes Beruf", *Gesammelte Aufsätze zur Kirchengeschichte* (Tübingen: JCB Mohr, 1928), III, pp. 189–219, considerably expanded by Robert L. Calhoun in *Work and Vocation*, ed. by John Oliver Nelson (New York: Harper & Brothers, 1954), pp. 85–115.

7. Richard Baxter, *Christian Directory* (1678 ed.), vol. 1, p. 336b. Quoted in R. H. Tawney, *Religion and the Rise of Capitalism* (New York: Harcourt, Brace & World, Inc., 1926) p. 242.

8. Ibid., p. 106.

9. Further elaboration of Calvin's economic ethic may be found in Ernst Troeltsch, *The Social Teaching of the Christian Church*, tr. by Olive Wyon (New York: Harper Torchbook, 1960), vol. 2, pp. 641ff.

10. Perry Miller, *The New England Mind: The Seventeenth Century*, p. 3, cited in Ahlstrom, *A Religious History*, p. 135.

11. The phrase is Tawney's from whom I take this whole exposition of Calvinist and Puritan economic virtues, *Rise of Capitalism*, pp. 110ff. and 227ff.

Chapter 2   American Puritans and the Great Awakening, pp. 16–23

1. Uriah Oakes, *New England Pleaded With* (1673), p. 49, quoted in Ahlstrom, *A Religious History*, p. 149.

2. Following Prof. McLoughlin's definition, an awakening is a culture-wide event, not merely a religious happening.

3. *Thoughts on the Revival of Religion in New England*, in *Works*, III, p. 314-315, quoted in Robert Handy, *A Christian America* (New York: Oxford, 1971), p. 21.

4. Tawney, *Rise of Capitalism*, p. 10.

5. Ibid., p. 10,11.

6. John Locke, *Concerning Civil Government, Second Essay* (1690), ch. IX, para. 124, *Great Books of the Western World*, vol. 35, ed. Robert M. Hutchins, (Chicago: Encyclopaedia Brittannica, Inc., 1952), p. 53.

7. Ahlstrom, *A Religious History*, p. 282.

8. Ibid., p. 349.

Chapter 3 The Second Great Awakening, pp. 24–34

1. Wm. G. McLoughlin, Jr., *Modern Revivalism: Charles Grandison Finney to Billy Graham* (New York: Ronald Press, 1959), p. 8.
2. Marty, *Righteous Empire*, p. 38; Winthrop C. Hudson, *Religion in America*, 2nd Ed. (New York: Charles Scribner's Sons, 1973), pp. 129, 130; Handy, *Christian America*, p. 27.
3. Beecher's autobiography was published by Harvard University Press, Cambridge, Mass.
4. My treatment of Finney is deeply indebted to Prof. McLoughlin. See also Neill Q. Hamilton, *Charles Grandison Finney, Two Problems in Evangelism*, unpublished Th.M. dissertation, Princeton Theol. Seminary, Princeton, N.J. 1953.
5. Charles G. Finney, *Lectures on Revivals of Religion*, (New York: Fleming H. Revell Co., 1868), p. 12.
6. Ibid., p. 290.
7. Handy, *Christian America*, p. 63.
8. Cited in McLoughlin, *Modern Revivalism*, p. 146.
9. I suppose it is unfair to blame that on Finney.
10. Quoted in Marty, *Righteous Empire*, p. 103.

Chapter 4 The Third Awakening, pp. 35–57

1. McLoughlin, *Modern Revivalism*, pp. 10, 168.
2. Handy, *Christian America*, p. 64.
3. Tawney, *Rise of Capitalism*, pp. 55, 56.
4. Weber, *The Protestant Ethic*, p. 56.
5. Francis Wayland, *The Elements of Political Economy*, 1837.
6. Tawney, *Rise of Capitalism*, p. 267.
7. Marty, *Righteous Empire*, p. 108.
8. Tawney, *Rise of Capitalism*, p. 193.
9. Marty, *Righteous Empire*, pp. 107, 108.
10. *A Critical Period in American Religion, 1875–1900* (Philadelphia: Fortress, 1967), originally appeared in *Massachusetts Historical Society Proceedings*, LXIV, October 1930–June 1932, pp. 523–46.
11. Vernon L. Parrington, "The American Scene", in *Democracy and the Gospel of Wealth*, ed. Gail Kennedy (Boston, D.C. Heath and Co.) 1949, p. 31.
12. Agnes R. Burr, *Russell Conwell and His Work* (Philadelphia: The John C. Winston Co., 1917), p. 314.
13. Russell H. Conwell, *Acres of Diamonds* (New York: Harper & Bros., 1915), p. 21.
14. Quoted in *Ethics in a Business Society*, eds. Marquis W. Childs, and Douglass Cater (New York: Harper & Bros., 1954), p. 137.

15. "Economy in Small Things," *Plymouth Pulpit*, New Series, III 1874–75, p. 263, quoted in Henry F. May, *Protestant Churches in Industrial America* (New York: Harper & Bros., 1948), p. 69.
16. Wm. Lawrence, "The Relation of Wealth to Morals," Gail Kennedy, ed., *Gospel of Wealth*, p. 69.
17. Andrew Carnegie, "Wealth," *North American Review*, 148, June 1889, p. 664, quoted in Kennedy, ibid., p. 8.
18. Handy, *Christian America*, p. 110.
19. For all my information about Moody, I am indebted to Prof. McLoughlin, *Modern Revivalism*, p. 166.
20. Conversation reported in introduction to Henry F. Drummond, *D.L. Moody*, 1900, pp. 24, 25, 28, 30, 32; cited in McLoughlin, *Modern Revivalism*, p. 276.
21. The scholarly response to new learning's challenge to the conventional view was led by the Princeton theologians Hodge and Warfield. Warfield's works on the subject are collected in *The Inspiration and Authority of the Bible*, ed. Samuel G. Craig (Philadelphia: Presbyterian and Reformed Publishing House, 1948).

    A recent survey question submitted to Protestants reads: "Scripture is the inspired and inerrant Word of God, not only in matters of faith, but also in historical, geographical and other secular matters." 71% of laity agreed. Hoge, *Division in the Protestant House*, p. 150.
22. Parrington, "The American Scene," p. 33.
23. This sketch of Gladden comes from May, *Protestant Churches*, pp. 171–76, and Ahlstrom, *A Religious History*, pp. 794–795.
24. Washington Gladden, *Applied Christianity*, Boston, 1886, pp. 135–36, 52, quoted in May, *Protestant Churches*, p. 173.
25. Marty, *Righteous Empire*, p. 186.
26. McLoughlin, *Modern Revivalism*, p. 330.
27. Marty, *Righteous Empire*, p. 183.
28. Quoted in McLoughlin, *Modern Revivalism*, p. 398.
29. Ibid., p. 334.
30. Ibid., p. 434.
31. Handy, *Christian America*, p. 164.
32. Marty, *Righteous Empire*, p. 152.

Chapter 5 The Aftermath of the Third Awakening, pp. 58–68

1. Richard Niebuhr, Francis Miller, and Wilhelm Pauck, *The Church Against the World* (Chicago: Willett, Clark & Co., 1935).
2. Ibid., p. 102.

3. Ibid., pp. 123, 124.
4. Ibid., p. 69.
5. *World Tomorrow*, XVII, April, 1a, 1934, quoted in Donald B. Meyer, *The Protestant Search for Political Realism, 1919-1941* (Berkeley: Univ. of Cal. Press, 1960), p. 220.
6. Ibid., p. 445, note 27. The difficulty of Richard Niebuhr's handling of the Kingdom of God in America, was that he never made clear what he "would do with the perfectionism rampant in that tradition."
7. Ibid., p. 403.
8. Martin Marty, *The New Shape of American Religion* (New York: Harper & Bros., 1958).
9. Quoted in Ahlstrom, *A Religious History*, p. 954.
10. For a summary of Graham's message see McLoughlin, *Modern Revivalism*, pp. 508ff., pp. 520, 521.
11. Ibid., p. 520.
12. Harmonial religion is Ahlstrom's phrase for pieties of well being that "flow from a person's rapport with the cosmos." *A Religious History*, p. 1019.
13. Jonathan Edwards, *A History of the Work of Redemption* (New York: American Tract Society, N.D.).
14. Ibid., p. 451.
15. Finney, *Revival Lectures*, p. 289.

PART II/*The Recovery of the Protestant Adventure*

Chapter 6   Dealing With the Demons, pp. 71–105

1. Karl Barth, *Church Dogmatics*, vol. 4, "The Doctrine of Reconciliation," Part Two (Edinburgh: T. & T. Clark, 1958), pp. 533–53.
2. For the rise of the apocalyptic see Neill Q. Hamilton, "The Dawn of the World to Come", in *Jesus for A No-God World* (Philadelphia: Westminster, 1968), pp. 11–42.
3. Martin Hengel, *Judaism and Hellenism* (Philadelphia: Fortress, 1974), vol. 1, p. 176.
4. For an explanation of redaction criticism see: Norman Perrin *What is Redaction Criticism?* (Philadelphia: Fortress, 1971); Joachim Rohde, *Rediscovering the Teaching of the Evangelists* (Philadelphia: Westminster, 1968).
5. Gunther Bornkamm, "The Stilling of the Storm in Matthew"; in Bornkamm, Barth, and Held, *Tradition and Interpretation in Matthew* (Philadelphia: Westminster, 1963), pp. 52–57.

6. Howard C. Kee, "The Terminology of Mark's Exorcism Stories," *New Testament Studies*, 14, 1968, p. 235.

7. Kee, "Exorcism Stories," p. 237.

8. Job 26:12; 2 Sam. 22:16; Ps. 104:7, 18:16, 106:9; Is. 17:13; Nahum 1:4; Is. 50:2. Kee, "Exorcism Stories," p. 236.

9. *Max Weber on Charisma and Institution Building*, ed. S.N. Eisenstadt (Chicago: Univ. Chicago Press, 1968), especially "The Nature of Charismatic Authority and Its Routinization," pp. 48–65, and the introductory essay by the editor.

10. Max Weber, *The Sociology of Religion*, trans. Ephraim Fischoff (Boston: Beacon Press, 1963), pp. 220ff.

11. Weber, *The Protestant Ethic*, p. 49.

12. Ibid., p. 182.

13. Ibid., p. 181.

14. This section builds on the insights of Thomas Luckmann, *The Invisible Religion* (New York: Macmillan, 1967).

15. Hoge, *Division*, p. 118.

16. Luckmann, *Invisible Religion*, p. 97.

17. Bryan R. Wilson, *Magic and the Millennium* (New York: Harper & Row, 1973), pp. 24, 25.

18. For an interpretation of the Jesus of the miracle tradition as a hellenistic miracle worker, see Helmut Koester, "One Jesus and Four Primitive Gospels," in *Trajectories through Early Christianity*, eds. James M. Robinson and Helmut Koester (Philadelphia: Fortress, 1971), pp. 187–93. For a refutation of this interpretation see H. Kee, *Community of the New Age* (Philadelphia: Westminster, 1977), pp. 23–30.

19. Ahlstrom, *A Religious History*, p. 1019.

Chapter 7 Discipleship, pp. 106–143

1. Johannes Weiss, *Jesus' Proclamation of the Kingdom of God* (Philadelphia: Fortress, 1971).

2. Kee, *Community*, pp. 106ff.

3. See James J. Robinson, *The Problem of History in Mark* (London: S.C.M. Press, 1957).

4. Harvey Cox, *The Seduction of the Spirit* (New York: Simon and Schuster, 1973), p. 84. Prof. Cox judges participatory planning to be the key to the emergence of the "city of light."

5. Following Rudolph Bultmann, *History of the Synoptic Tradition* (New York: Harper & Row, 1963), p. 23.

6. Bonhoeffer made the mistake of trying to draw from this and other "call" stories a model for a kind of blind obedience that

simply responds to the sheer authority of Jesus—"the obligation of single-minded, literal obedience." Dietrich Bonhoeffer, *The Cost of Discipleship* (New York: Macmillan, 1963).

7. Marty, *Righteous Empire*, p. 88.

8. Horace Bushnell, *Christian Nurture* (Grand Rapids, MI: Baker Book House, 1979, reprint of 1861 ed.), p. 10.

9. Barth, *Dogmatics*, vol. 4, 2, p. 553.

10. Martin Hengel, *Nachfolge und Charisma* (Berlin: Verlag Alfred Töpelmann, 1968), p. 80 (my translation); followed by Kee, *Community*, p. 87.

11. This is the conclusion for example of Schulz, who finds that the imitation of Christ naturally displaced discipleship after the passing of the historical Jesus. After the fact, believers can only imitate the example of the Jesus of the ministry. "Follow" only applies to the historical Jesus "in ihrer irdische Existensweise." Anselm Schulz, *Nachfolgen und Nachahmen* (München: Kösel Verlag, 1962), p. 64. See Gerhard Kittel "akoloutheo," *Theologisches Wörterbuch zum Neuen Testament*, vol. 1 (Stuttgart: Verlag Von W. Kohlhammer, 1933), p. 215, who also emphasizes the exclusive application to the historical Jesus. Similarly, Hans Dieter Betz, *Nachfolge und Nachahmung Jesu Christi in Neuen Testament* (Tubingen: J.G.B. Mohr [Paul Steinbeck], 1967).

12. For the history of redaction criticism see Rohde, *Teaching of the Evangelists*.

13. Robinson and Koester put Mark and John on the same gospel trajectory. *Trajectories*, pp. 188, 189, 267, 268.

14. Hans Conzelmann, *The Theology of St. Luke* (New York: Harper & Row, 1960).

15. Bornkamm showed the way with his essay on the "Stilling of the Storm," available in Bornkamm, Barth, and Held, *Tradition and Interpretation*, pp. 52–57.

16. Jack Dean Kingsbury, "The Verb Akolouthein ("To Follow") as an Index of Matthew's View of his Community," *Journal of Biblical Literature*, vol. 97, no. 1, March 1978, pp. 57–73.

17. Kee, *Community*, p. 110.

18. Willie Marxsen, *Introduction to the New Testament* (Philadelphia: Fortress, 1968); Perrin, *N.T. Introduction*, p. 150.

19. Eduard Schweizer, *The Good News According to Mark* (Atlanta: John Knox Press, 1970), p. 366. Vincent Taylor, *The Gospel According to St. Mark* (New York: Macmillan, 1966), pp. 608–609.

20. A comparison of the resurrection appearances of Matthew and Luke does not yield a common Marcan core.

21. Martin Dibelius, *From Tradition to Gospel* (New York: Charles Scribner's Sons, 1934), p. 14.
22. Ibid., p. 230.
23. Bultmann, *Synoptic Tradition*, p. 346.
24. Ibid., p. 348.
25. Willi Marxsen, *Mark the Evangelist* (Nashville: Abingdon Press, 1969), pp. 117–50.
26. Marxsen, *N.T. Introduction*, p. 138.
27. K. Reploh, *Markus-Lehrer der Gemeinde* (Stuttgart: Verlag Katholische Bibelwerk, 1969).
28. "Galilee" is always found in Mark in editorial passages. Marxsen, *N.T. Introduction*, p. 138. Mark 1:9, 14, 16, 28, 39; 3:7; 8:31; 9:30; 14:28; 16:7.
29. Ibid., p. 141.
30. Kee, *Community*, p. 95.
31. "The one architectural feature that stands out, Mark has placed at the center of his gospel (Mk. 9:2ff.), the eschatological vision of Jesus' exaltation at God's right hand." Kee, *Community*, p. 75.
32. Ibid., p. 138.
33. The passages are: Mark 4:1, 2, 10–13, and 33, 34. Prof. Jeremias has made a thorough analysis of the chapter. Verses 11 and 34 are clearly the creation of the Marcan editor. He attached the saying in verse 12 which is a paraphrase of Is. 6:9f already in use in the synagogue of his day. It is important for my exposition that the editor also appended the parables of the lamp and bushel, and of the measure. They commission him to reveal the meaning of parables by writing his book. Joachim Jeremias, *The Parables of Jesus* (New York: Charles Scribner's Sons, 1963), pp. 13ff.
34. For the source of this idea in the apocalyptic stream represented by 4 Ezra, 1 Enoch, 2 Baruch, and Qumran, see the unpublished Drew doctoral dissertation directed by my colleague Prof. Lala Kalyan Dey: Priscilla C. Patten, *Parable and Secret*, 1976.
35. Ibid., pp. 64–71.
36. Ibid., p. 79.
37. Mark 1:35, 36; 3:31–35; 4:10–20; 4:33–34; 5:37–43; 7:17–23; 9:2–13; 9:28, 29; 9:30–32; 10:10–12.
38. Similar instances at Mark 5:40; 11:11; 14:17; 14:33.
39. Also 14:14"... to eat the passover with my disciples..."
40. Similar verbs at 14:3 "die with" and 15:41 "came up with"
41. Wilhelm Wuellner, *The Meaning of "Fishers of Men"* (Philadelphia: Westminster, 1967).

42. Against Wuellner, ibid., p. 231.
43. Taylor, *St. Mark*, p. 284.
44. I base this interpretation on the fact that the editor used "the Lord" and "Jesus" interchangeably in verses 19 and 20. With Ernst Haenchen, *Der Weg Jesu*, 2nd ed. (Berlin: Walter de Gruyter and Co., 1968), p. 195 and against Taylor, *St. Mark*, p. 285.
45. F.W. Beare put it exactly right, "Mark himself passes over it lightly." *The Earliest Records of Jesus* (Nashville: Abingdon Press, 1962), p. 125.
46. Contra Hengel, *Nachfolge und Charisma*, and Schulz, *Nachfolgen*.
47. Weber, *The Protestant Ethic*, 1958.
48. William S. Coffin, Jr., *Once to Every Man, A Memoir* (New York: Atheneum, 1977), p. 146.

Chapter 8 Discipleship in Political Perspective, pp. 144–182

1. For analysis see J. Lamprecht, *Die Redaktion der Markus-Apokalypse* (Rome: Pontifical Biblical Institute, 1967), (Analecta Biblica 28). Regardless of the particular analysis, the chapter has long been considered composite by scholars.
2. The editor's style is evident in verse 1; "and", "come out", historic present of "said", Mark's most frequent address "teacher"; verse 2: "And", "see"; double negative for *not left* and *not thrown* down.
3. Josephus, *The Jewish War*, H. St. J. Thackeray (Cambridge: Harvard Univ. Press, 1961), Bk. 2, pp. 538f., lines 562–64.
4. Fulfillment of Scripture was one of the main sources of Mark's theology. Scriptural allusions and quotations undergird the whole, but especially the last third of the book. See Kee, *Community*, pp. 45ff.
5. For editorial creation of the predictions, see N. Perrin, *Christology and a Modern Pilgrimage*, (Society of Biblical Literature, 1971), pp. 14–30, ed. Hans Dieter Betz.
    For editorial creation of the Passion Narrative, see Kee, *Community*, pp. 30–32.
6. 8:27–33 is a composition of the editor combining a Baptist Elijah prophet tradition (vv. 27:1–28, // 6:14, 15), a confession of Peter (v. 29), a prediction of the passion (v. 31 // 19:31; 19:33), and the saying about Satan (vs. 32b, 33).
7. Strach-Billerbeck, *Kommentar zum Neuen Testament aus Talmud und Midrash*, vol. 1, p. 835ff. (München: C.H. Beck, 1922).
8. W. Bauer, *Griechisch-Deutsches Wörterbuch*, ed. Arndt and Gingrich (Chicago: Univ. of Chicago Press, 1952).

9. "He (Simon) sought the good of his nation; his rule was pleasing to them as was the glory shown to him, all his days. To crown all his glories..." 1 Macc. 14:4, 5, cf. 1 Macc. 10:58 for the same meaning.

10. W. Marxsen, *The Resurrection of Jesus of Nazareth*, (Philadelphia: Fortress, 1970).

11. "We cannot abide Niebuhr's line that the Sermon on the Mount is good for our personal lives but impractical for affairs of state.
    We are confused by the position of some Quakers and Anabaptists. They say, for example, that it is okay for the state to use violence because the state isn't Christian. (Of course, the state *isn't* Christian but sin is sin whether committed by Christians or non-Christians.) We get so upset we become incoherent when someone (say Jimmy Carter) suggests that morality and human rights are important but so are America's economic and military interests. (What's right is right, blast it.)"
    John Alexander, "In search of who we are. A look at the 'fundamentals of radical Christianity.'" *The Other Side*, July 1978, p. 12.

12. "What H.R. Niebuhr would do with the perfectionism rampant in that tradition, and criticized by his brother, was never clear." Donald B. Meyer, *The Protestant Search for Political Reality, 1919–41* (Berkeley: U.C. Press, 1960). Note 27, p. 445.

13. "We are prevented from interpreting the Fourth Gospel as a wholly conversionist document..."
    "The Christian life seems to be possible only to the few." H. Richard Niebuhr, *Christ and Culture*, (New York: Harper & Bros., 1951), p. 204.

14. In the measure that Troeltsch misses this point, a chronicling of the social teaching of the churches is beside the point.

Chapter 9 Son-of-man Discipleship in Practice, pp 183–211

1. As the public party regularly reminds us, the Old Testament is full of explicit injunctions to do justice as well as to love mercy and walk humbly with God. The difficulty is that the prophets of justice in the Old Testament were addressing a confessing community, which our nation is not. Furthermore, the adoption of an apocalyptic viewpoint makes prophetic justice seem no longer applicable in so fallen a world.

2. Alexander, "In Search of Who We Are," p. 14.

3. John G. Gager, *Kingdom and Community* (Englewood Cliffs, N.J.: Prentice-Hall, Inc., 1975), p. 131.

4. Ibid.

5. Kittel, *Wöerterbuch*, vol. 4 (1942), "martus", p. 511.

6. *Webster's New Collegiate Dictionary* (Springfield, Mass.: Merriam Co., 1975).

Index

Also available from The Seabury Press:

The Inflated Self: Human Illusions and the Biblical Call to Hope
by David G. Myers

The Broken Covenant: American Civil Religion in Time of Trial
by Robert N. Bellah

An Interpretation of Christian Ethics
by Reinhold Niebuhr